MW00721002

Flipped Out?

Want to Achieve

Sustainable

Real Estate

Success?

Mike Sanderson with Jim LeVine

Mike Sanderson with Jim LeVine
Sanderson Publishing, Inc.

Flipped Out?
Want to achieve sustainable real estate success?
©2010 by Mike Sanderson with Jim LeVine

Printed in China
Written with the assistance of Jim LeVine, Ph.D.
Cover Design: Mike Portillo, Mana Brand Marketing
Interior Design and Page Layout: Doris Bruey

Publisher's Cataloging-in-Publication
(provided by Quality Books, Inc.)

Mike Sanderson with Jim LeVine
Flipped Out?
Want to achieve sustainable real estate success?
/Mike Sanderson with Jim LeVine
p. cm.
Includes index.
Library of Congress Control Number: 2010902254
ISBN: 978-0-9842902-0-8

WHAT PEOPLE SAY ABOUT MIKE SANDERSON

I have had the pleasure of knowing Mike Sanderson. There are few like him. Mike encompasses everything that is necessary to be highly successful. His people skills, his knowledge of real estate and construction, and most importantly his limitless view of possibility put Mike in a league of his own.

In the world of entrepreneurship there are no guarantees. Having the ability to find the opportunity in all markets and economies takes a large reference of experience. Mike and his family have been at this for a very long time. The learning curve on so many things could be cut short dramatically by spending some time at the feet of this man. His perspective and expertise are solid and timeless. His honesty and ethics are what makes a business stand the test of time.

Without any reservation, I would recommend spending any amount of time and money you have to learn from this man. You and your tomorrow will not regret it.

Greg Pinneo
Real Estate Entrepreneur, Teacher, and Speaker
Reach Returns Inc., Co-Owner

I have had the privilege of working with Mike since 1994. We have worked on many real estate projects and transactions over the years. Mike has a unique ability to envision the potential in any project, while carefully considering the risks that come with the rewards. Mike is very systematic in his approach to business. He knows what works, and what doesn't. With his knowledge and vision, Mike has turned several challenging projects into profitable business ventures over the years. He has always demonstrated a high level of integrity and willingness to create the win-win deal for those involved. I have witnessed time and time again how Mike's formula has proven to be successful and profitable!

Rob Graham
Keller Williams Realty

I have been Mike's architect on a number of his projects and as our professional relationship grew I found a person I not only wanted to work with but I found a guy I wanted to call a friend. From a profession aspect; I have made that first walk through a new project with Mike and seen his wheels in action. With his years of experience, he is able to stare at a pile of rubble and literally describe to me a brand new house amongst all the debris. The genius with Mike is that he doesn't pretend to know it all and allows people he works with to contribute ideas and thoughts when he is unsure of the best way to go. This teamwork approach on all levels of development, allows Mikes' projects to be very successful in the end both financially and for his residents. Mike's desire to do things the right way in business formed the basis for a great friendship. When I bought my first fixer-upper, Mike was willing to give his personal time and make that same walk through my house and give me advice and ideas. Over the years we have found many opportunities to collaborate on projects and he continues to impress me with dedication to better peoples lives by providing them with a place to call home.

Mat Bergman
Project Manager, BCRA
Tacoma, Washington

Mike Sanderson Jr. has been one of the most positive and dynamic individuals I've worked with in my years of real estate development. I found Mike's word to be more binding than contracts I've had with other investor / partners in the past.

We were working together as the housing industry took its downward turn. When it came time to discuss strategy in dealing with the market, Mike always greeted me with a smile and a positive attitude that helped me stay motivated.

It wasn't so much his vast experience and knowledge in real estate and finance that saved our projects, as his spontaneous ingenuity. I'm looking forward to our continuing working relationship and would certainly recommend him in any capacity to anyone considering working with him in the future as well.

Larry Wagner
New Atlantis
Puyallup, Washington

The first time I met Mike he went out of his way to offer his time, knowledge, and experience "anytime", and he has lived up to this promise ever since. He took the time to meet with me at a home I was considering, walked through the home with me and thoroughly went over the pro's and con's of taking on the project. He even provided some ideas he would apply if it were his. Integrity Matters in all relationships and Mike is truly a man of his word. All who know him are blessed.

Jim Hagen

Mike Sanderson is my neighbor and friend. I know first hand how dependable, honest and hard working he is. He has been very successful with his business enterprises… a charter fishing boat and several real estate ventures. Mike is very knowledgeable concerning property and business issues and I would recommend him to anyone needing guidance.

Chuck O'Farrell
Tacoma, Washington

I have known the Sanderson family for some fifteen years and have assisted them with accounting, tax, estate and other tax planning issues during this time and prepared their various tax returns as required.

Their business started as a real estate rental company where they have owned, managed and maintained over 100 properties in and around the Tacoma, Washington area. The businesses and companies have expanded to include real estate development and lending money for loans secured by real estate.

But the basic core business during this time has been rental properties and this has probably included every possible rental problem and opportunity imaginable.

I have known Mike during this time and he has been willing to get the job done whatever the task might be, ranging from dealing with customers, vendors, subcontractors and various government agencies. He has always maintained a very high work ethic, coupled with professionalism at every level. His character, honesty, knowledge and experience, by learning the business from the ground up has gained him great respect.

So I Thank him for the opportunity to be involved with him and his family and the various businesses over the last fifteen years and can recommend this book because of his vast business knowledge and accomplishments.

Duane E. Anderson, CPA

Mike Sanderson Jr., what can I say? I worked closely with Mike, his father, and office manager for many years. In that time I have seen Mike grow in his awareness and understanding of what it takes to own and run a successful rental home business, versus being self-employed in a business, that among other things, rents houses. Mike's integrity and honesty were evident in his willingness to turn his attention not only outward, as he expanded his knowledge of business and the industry, but inward as well, as he delved into investigating his own management and ultimately leadership skills. Enjoy his shared journey.

Judith Lerner
E-Myth Worldwide, Inc.

Mike Sanderson has been a great help to me as I grew my Real Estate Investing (REI) business. Mike is very knowledgeable, and, by nature, an exceptionally helpful person. Mike constantly explained things to me in simple terms and I never felt foolish when talking to him.

Mike is my go to guy any time I did not know the answer to a problem. At all times Mike knew the answer or he had a contact that he recommended who helped me solve the issue. More often than not at far lower prices than I could have done it myself.

Following Mike's guidance was continuously beneficial in saving time and money. One time I failed to listen to him and decided to do it myself and not hire the consultant Mike recommended. In the end all the extra work I did failed to save me any money and took six months longer than if I would have hired his consultant.

As a REI of over 18 years, I can honestly say, "If you are an experienced REI or just a beginner you can find no better mentor or coach than Mike Sanderson."

Paul Hemming
Tacoma, WA

I can certainly confirm that I have worked with Mike Sanderson for some years now, during which time he has provided my business with excellent support in the area of our rental business. Mike is one of the few that I can say that works with a high level of integrity and honesty and with a level of experience surpassed by none. My wife and I have been in business for the last 15 years. Over that time Mike has been the best source of true advice that really works. His many years of experience with the ability to pass it on to us has been a major factor in our success.

I can confidently recommend Mike Sanderson as a solid and credible person who is in the trenches and knows how this business works inside and out.

Scott Williams
Unity Property Solutions, Inc.

In the years that I have known Mike Sanderson, I have come to count on his excellent advice. He is very honest and will tell it like it is while still making sure you are comfortable with the results. Mike has a great ability to make you feel like yours is the only project he is working on. Mike will show an incredible pride and confidence in his business but if you want to see real passion you have to get his on Fishing Boat. I have enjoyed all of my dealings with Mike regardless of the field.

Ezra McCallister
District Manager, Sterling Jewelers

Mike Sanderson is on of those people I look up to and call when I need to know something about rental property. I have been in the business for over 20 years as an agent and my husband and I have rental property of our own. I have never seen an operation run so smoothly as Mike's, in fact, we are striving to be like him! Mike has been very generous with his time and support. I am so excited to know that his information will be able to be used by many people who are looking to get ahead - not the get rich quick schemers - the true salt of the earth type of people who want a lasting and rewarding way to generate income. Thanks for all of your support and encouragement Mike!

Michelle Broderson, Associate Broker
Wilson Realty Exchange, Inc.
Vice President, The Bravo Group, Inc.

I wish to express my sincerest appreciation for the opportunity to work with you on the sales of your recent homes. It's no wonder you've accomplished so much in the rental property and Real Estate markets!

Your knowledge, expertise and timely follow through contributed greatly to the success of your transactions.

Best wishes on your book and coaching business efforts.

I'm confident that your integrity and business acumen will be well received.

Thanks you once again for all of your hard work. Hats off to you!

Dan Marks, Associate Broker
John L. Scott Real Estate

TABLE OF CONTENTS

DEDICATION

I have been blessed to have many mentors and people who have supported my crazy endeavors over the span of my life and are grateful to all of them:

. . . My Grandfather who took me under his wing when I was ten years old and put me to work on the charter fishing boats. He taught me the value of hard work and the skill of working with people from all walks of life.

. . . My Father has always been there to guide me along the way. Working with him all these years has truly been a blessing. He has taught me so much by his example and his support.

. . . Glenda's 15-year devotion to working with us has been more of a challenge than she expected. Without her our operation does not get to where it is today. She truly is the third leg of our stool.

. . . My Bride, Janine, whose love and support has been instrumental in so many of my undertakings including this book. Her incredible faith in me is inspiring everyday.

. . . Our 5 teenage children – Nickle, Shelby, Quinn, Kurt, and Nikki, who have the distinct way of keeping me grounded and remembering what my #1 job really is.

. . . My office and maintenance staff, suppliers, subcontractors, professionals, buyers and sellers I have worked with over the many years. I have learned from all of you.

. . . Jim LeVine, my coach, who is directly responsible for getting this all into print. His ability to drag enough information out of me to have it make sense is uncanny. It has been a privilege to have him guide me through this project and become my friend.

FORWARD

I come from a land not far from where you are right now. I live and work in a place that probably looks very similar to the neighborhoods you drive through everyday. I suppose I deal with the same economic challenges that you face in your area. And I'm guessing that there is not much difference between our locals and your locals -- that is there is probably not much difference in the opportunities available.

I say this so that you and I can get on the same page right away. I know the challenges that are out there today in my community. I not only know them, I live with these challenges everyday: the lack of institutional financing, mortgage rules changing all the time, unrealistic asking prices, and enough government regulations to choke a horse, just to name a few. So what is a guy supposed to do you ask? Well, the answer to this question is an easy one -- you look for the opportunities that exist or make your own. Do smart business and keep going. That's what I do.

I've always joked that I'm not smart enough to quit during rough times. The fact of the matter is that I don't want to quit. Making it through the tough times is what separates the men from the boys, as they say; and my self-confidence is in tact enough as a result of my long apprenticeship and positive experiences in this business to believe that I'm good enough to make it anytime, anywhere. My father told me many times that most anybody can make money in the good times, but it's the tough times that will be the real test of how well I've learned my lessons. I'm pretty sure we are seeing a great example of his assessment in today's economy. The easy days of everyone making money in real estate hand over fist are gone for now. They may not return for quite some time again, and I am o.k. with that. Those of us that are left are the professionals -- the survivors if you will. The new investors coming in today's market are doing so a little more cautiously such as putting a lot more emphasis on their education. This is what I want for you -- to be knowledgeable about what it is that you are getting into. Learn what you can and hire the right people to help you. Hey, that would be me!

So I ask you, when you look around your neighborhood, what do you see? When you're driving in the neighborhoods around your kid's school what do you see? Do you see opportunity? I do.

Now lets deal with the buzzword of the current times – "FINANCING". I can tell you in all certainty that this book is not about financing; nor is it about the latest and greatest get rich quick scheme.

. . . this book is not about financing . . .

I apologize for that outburst! Forgive me. I was talking about financing. The financing tools that are required in this business are ever changing. This is a fact. The way I financed acquisitions differed greatly from one project to another and differed greatly over time. Banking options are not the same as they once were as little as two years ago -- they are much more limited now. The requirements that the conventional financing world has placed on investors have made acquisitions more difficult. With the financial world on another of its extreme pendulum swings at present, this time to the side of needing to be ridiculously perfect before one can qualify for a mortgage, it is time for some other financing tools to come into prominence. Seller financing is making a comeback from years in the closet. This type of financing was very popular in the 1970's when my father was starting his real estate career and is very viable again. Private financing from individuals that are tired of being beat up in the stock market is another viable option right now. Discussing these couple of options is just my way of showing that building a viable real estate business is possible in the current conditions as well as before. There is no doubt in my mind that me and my team could do now again what we did then, the difference being that the financing procedure would look a little different. The important thing for you to understand is that no matter what the financial world is going through, all the other elements of this business remain the same -- the house, the residents, and the systems you must have in place to make it all work.

So do yourself a favor and read this book for the reason I wrote it -- to educate and open your mind to the rental business as a robust business with a lot of possibilities. Don't discount the information within these covers as old news. That little devil guy that sits on your shoulder and says "this won't work in today's market" or "I can't find the money to do that" -- that little devil will keep you sleeping in bed all your days if you let him. Read this book thinking about all the possibilities it opens up for you and the way to build what you want. Think of financing in the way my father taught me years ago. "If the deal is good enough, you can find the money".

. . . educate and open your mind to the rental business as a robust business with a lot of possibilities . . .

So who needs to read this book? Everyone who is involved in the rental real estate world from the beginner who needs to know what you are getting into; to the novice who wants to go to the next level ; to the pro who knows the value of picking up those one or two little tips that will help their business.

INTRODUCTION

Who Am I And Why Am I Writing This Book?

Would You Like To Own A Business That Warren Buffet May Love?

Kind of a stupid question, huh? Who wouldn't like to own one of these companies? And what kind of company would this be?

Well, owning a business that one of the best investors of all times – billionaire, Warren Buffet may love to own would probably mean that this is one of the few great companies that is well managed and producing great profits, quarter-after-quarter, year-after-year, and decade-after-decade.

Of course, this is a very high standard of quality as far as companies go if Warren Buffet likes it. It probably means that this business is one of the best of the best. And as long as we're talking about the best of the best, we can probably infer that a number of the following qualities apply:

The Business Warren Buffet May Love To Own:

- . . . is highly profitable with good margins
- . . . is reliably profitable year-in-year-out, in good times and bad
- . . . has a product that is in high demand and is a "must have". With this in mind, the business is probably fulfilling fundamental human needs: food, shelter or clothing -- needs that are never-ending, no-matter-what, no-matter how, no-matter-who
- . . . has steadily growing free cash flows -- unburdened cash flows available to be spent on anything a business requires
- . . . has passive, residual income, meaning it's earning money when you're not on the job – when you are sleeping, on vacation, and involved in your hobbies

- . . . has great management that requires minimal attention because of the high quality work they do
- . . . has substantial government tax benefits
- . . . has appreciating value that far outstrips it's depreciating value
- . . . has a high proportion of non-destructible assets
- . . . has products that are easy to understand
- . . . all parts of the business are well organized and so efficiently operated that they are kind of boring
- . . . has multiple options for earning income
- . . . has multiple options for selling it's products
- . . . has tangible, physical products
- . . . can be reproduced as a business anywhere
- . . . provides an important social benefit
- . . . makes sense as a business if the numbers work

Guess what? My name is Mike Sanderson; I'm a very successful real estate investor; and I have a business Warren Buffet may love to own.

How do I know? Because my business fits every single criteria on the list I've just described . . . and then some because it has:

- sustainability;
  - year-round all-weather, all-season success
  - products that are always in demand -- housing
  - products that fulfill simple, classic needs -- shelter
- positive, unburdened free cash flow;
- high relative liquidity – ability to sell off quickly, if and when desired;
- low maintenance cost with few surprises;
- good appreciation based on buying low and selling higher
- multiple investment opportunities; and

- systems are in place and working so that you don't have to spend all of your time engaged in paying attention to it.
- tax benefits that are not available in other kinds of investments

But You Wouldn't Know How Successful I Am Because:

- My business is for the most part invisible;
- I have a business model that few other people who call themselves real estate investors follow; and
- I have a lifestyle that doesn't resemble anything you've seen or heard about as being associated with a successful real estate investor.

Here's What I Have:

- . . . a 15 year old business that began well before it was popular to be in this business
- . . . 115 units
  - 85 single family homes and
  - 30 multi-family housing units
- . . . a business structured on the basis of a three legged stool --
  1. . . . finance (financing of acquisitions, property acquisition, negotiations);
  2. . . . building renovation (revenue enhancement, repairs, modernization); and
  3. . . . property management and maintenance
- . . . a 9 member staff that includes
  - Chairman of the Board –COB
  - Chief Executive Officer CEO
  - Chief Operations Officer – COO
  - Chief Financial Officer - CFO
  - Property Manager
  - Maintenance Manager
  - Bookkeeper
- . . . a business office
- . . . a base yard with shop, warehouse, parking for company vehicles used in property management and maintenance

- ... all income producing options open to us
  - long term appreciation
  - tax advantages
  - capital gains preferred tax treatment
  - substantial depreciation of my asset base
  - business deductibles
  - tax subsidized demand – renters subsidized by various government programs
- ... positive free cash flow
- ... immediate and long term selling options
  - purchase and sell
  - fully renovate and sell
  - fully renovate and rent
  - purchase, partially renovate, and sell
  - sell on option
  - purchase, trade, and exchange

Who am I?
- ... CEO, out of day-to-day management, on-call 24/7
- ... dependent upon management systems in place
- ... still hauling garbage
- ... still involved in the major decision making process
- ... still driving the neighborhoods
- ... not a member of a country club or yacht club
- ... intermittently involved in acquisition and renovation
- ... married, 5 kids
- ... still drive mostly Chevrolets

I am still very much involved in my business in a way that gives me the opportunity to have a great overview of the whole. The nature of our business is that I can become very active in it opportunistically at times, or significantly withdraw from it and let it operate almost on automatic pilot. I have set up my business to take advantage of periodic real estate cycles so that I am always doing well, in all of the various phases of the cycles. This is distinguished from many real estate investors, engaged in short term revenue generating techniques who only do well when the real estate market is going up.

Why Am I Writing This?

- … because my industry has been full of "Seminar" gurus for way too long. These seminar snake oil salesmen have given the real estate industry a bad name and have taken a lot of peoples' money for not much return. The majority of these "seminar experts" are just that. Experts in selling people a get rich quick fantasy and taking their money before running out of town. I believe in the value of education and it disgusts me to see people being taken advantage of with these "hurry to the back of the room" type of presentations. They do not have the years of experience nor are they still in the business like I am. My industry deserves better. I will give you better.

. . . My industry deserves better. I will give you better . . .

- . . . because I'm troubled that many so-called real estate investors are embracing the wrong business model and keep invading my world, messing things up
- . . . because I want to share what I've learned all of these years
- . . . because nobody ever has
- . . . and because some in my industry are termed "slumlords" who have the reputation of doing business in a selfish, unscrupulous manner – a reputation that has given the entire rental real estate industry an unfair bad rap

My Unique Qualifications And Those Of My Company

A lot of people call themselves real estate investors, but I know most have not reached the level of success that I currently enjoy. There are no doubt many reasons for this – chief among them is probably the fact that most investors don't have the capabilities that I and my team have, and they don't put in play a business model that my team and I have perfected over a period of 15 years.

As For Myself . . .

… I've built my career from the ground up for the past 27 years around a broad scope of training, experiences, and skills that complement the unique and simple real estate investment business model I follow. You might compare my preparation for the real estate investment business to the person who starts in the mailroom, and eventually works his way up to the top of a major corporation, learning all the jobs that contribute to the success of the organization along the way – because I've had them all. This depth of experience enables me to sense what's going on frequently before it's even described to me, because I've been there so many times before. I've done it all in the business model that I follow, and paid for my training many times over in missteps, wrong-turns, and trip-ups.

My interest in this career begin when I was 12 years old when my Dad asked me to participate in landscaping a housing project he was doing during my summer vacation. During my final year in high school at age 17, rather than go to college, I couldn't wait to begin working with Dad on his land development and housing projects, so I did –building, remodeling, and developing land in Washington. When I was 18, I spent a year in Alaska with my cousin and Dad working on building 4plex multi-family housing units. Just before I turned 18, I passed the Washington State Real Estate licensing exam so that I could have the necessary knowledge to buy and sell property.

I then spent over 8 years working for a heavy highway construction company grade-checking then supervising as a job foreman: the clearing and grubbing, staking, mass grading, landscaping and construction of roads, drainage ways, retaining walls, water holding tanks and underground utilities (storm sewer, sanitary sewer, phone, gas, electrical, cable television) for interstate highways, state highways, busy city streets, private roads, airports, prisons, and golf courses.

I then went back into house building on my own for a few years with a concentrated effort in the single family, first time home buyer's market. This worked out pretty well for me, but I still wanted more.

When my father, another team member and I got together and decided to focus on building a substantial rental home portfolio, things started to come together. I really enjoyed the years we have spent buying fixer-uppers, rehabilitating them, renting them out or selling them and developing our workflow systems to handle it all.

I got very good at taking a newly acquired fixer-upper and finding ways to increase its value, whether it was through updating and modernizing the floor plan, adding or redoing stairwells, or adding additional bedrooms. Because each home we acquired offered similar, yet unique challenges, I gravitated to getting deeply involved in this creative exercise so much so that it became the role everyone in our company looked to me to fulfill.

. . . I got very good at taking a newly acquired fixer-upper and finding ways to increase its value . . .

I also performed other roles including negotiating with realtors, owners, title companies, escrow agents, and bankers for acquisition of property; acquired permits from public agencies; worked with architects, civil engineers, wetlands experts, lawyers, interior designers, sound engineers, foundation engineers, structural engineers, permit specialists, contractors (roofers, surveyors, electricians, framers, plumbers, underground utility specialists, grading, painting, concrete, sheet rockers, flooring specialists, landscapers); suppliers (windows, lumber, flooring, hardware, cabinets, sash & doors, trim, trusses); direct marketing; sales negotiations through realtors; purchasing property at foreclosure sales; hard money lending; oversight of construction activity; and completion of subdivision development of single family homes, commercial property, mobile homes, and modular housing.   I'm certain I've forgotten to mention some subspecialty that I have worked with before. In addition, I have attended classes too numerous to remember on many of these professional topics.

All told so far, I have built around 50 new houses and well over 100 renovation projects, most of which our company still owns, manages and maintains. This deep background along with my extensive experience in site work, land and property development, real estate investment, property management and property maintenance makes me very unusual in the real estate development and investment field. There are many specialists in the field who are trained and experienced in one part or another of the field, but very few who are experienced in mostly all of them as I am.

. . . All told so far, I have built around 50 new houses and well over 100 renovation projects, most of which our company still owns, manages and maintains . . .

Needless to say, I have a very unique perspective about the real estate investment business that I think will benefit you to learn about. If you are going to be in this business, you need to know me!

As For My Team . . .

… we now have 7 employees who manage 115 rental properties consisting of 85 single-family homes and 30 multifamily units. This team has all of the skills that are needed to do all the functions that are required to administer, manage, and maintain all the property as well as take on the many functions that new projects require. The functions of these employees include administration, operations, property management, maintenance, accounting, acquisition, financing acquisition, negotiations, and renovations. In addition to these functions, we also have acquisition management, construction management, property management, and office management systems in place to enable us to operate quite efficiently.

We may be small, but we have all the staff and staff experience we need to handle just about anything the real estate investment business can throw our way. I am very proud of my team. Not only are their skills and experience very deep in land development, new home single family subdivision development, single family renovation development, administration, finance, property management, and property maintenance, but they are a well oiled machine that functions well together. I am deeply indebted to my team for enabling me to function, grow, and thrive. I could not have accomplished nor learned anywhere near as much as I've learned without them. If you are going to expand your business beyond four units, you are going to have to have a team. And if you are going to be in this business, you need to know my team!

As For The Business Model Of Our Team . . .

I said earlier that my business is for-the-most-part invisible. This is by-and-large true. We have an office and a warehouse located in a very ordinary, nondescript portion of Tacoma, Washington that you would have to know about in order to find. The majority of our properties are distributed throughout this neighborhood, with a few exceptions of properties that are spread out elsewhere. This is a blue-collar neighborhood where the average price of a single-family home goes for $150,000 - $200,000. We intentionally selected this price range of homes to work with to give us maximum flexibility. Higher prices limit flexibility by cutting off financing options, among other things.

. . . my business is for-the-most-part-invisible . . .

I also said earlier that I have a unique and simple business model that few other people who call themselves real estate investors follow. This is a long-term model with the following 14 key features:

The 14 Key Features of my unique and simple real estate investment business model:

1. … a focus on acquisition of low cost single family homes at beneficial times in opportunistic situations
2. … a focus on rental housing instead of resale housing
3. … a focus on families as residents instead of foot-loose singles
4. … purchase of below average, substandard fixer-uppers at bargain basement, below market prices – the ugliest homes in neighborhoods where the average home is of a lot better quality

5. … renovation primarily for the purpose of rental (as distinguished from sales). Rental renovations are intended to last a long time. Sales renovations are intended for making positive short-term impressions.
6. … significant renovation (as distinguished from cosmetic renovation) to increase rental revenue (Adding more bedrooms will do this)
7. … long-term rental with positive cash flow from day one of rent up (Revenues exceeding expenses)
8. … property management throughout the rental holding period (that could be a very long time –years and years)
9. … property maintenance throughout the rental holding period (that could be a very long time –years and years)
10. … use of a variety of financing instruments to purchase, leverage, and hold property prior to resale, including cash, seller carry-back loans, construction loans, 5 year balloon loans, and permanent 30 year fixed rate low interest loans
11. … avoidance of government loan programs to acquire and renovate property because of their "red" tape, non-business efficiency perspective
12. … ownership of property is held indefinitely until a sale is desired, an optimal pricing point is reached, or a long term tenant/resident makes a good offer
13. … ownership that maximizes the depreciation and other property management and maintenance tax benefits
14. … sales that optimize tax exposure

This business model enables a wide variety of income revenue opportunities to occur that I'll describe in more detail throughout the book. This array of choices provides many investment diversification benefits that increases my flexibility, lowers my risks and optimizes my returns.

*. . . **This business model enables a wide variety of income revenue opportunities to occur** . . .*

I have and do participate in other business models that include higher risk investments. I have engaged in these business models with the full knowledge of what I was getting into. Most have worked out well and a few haven't gone nearly as planned. I tell you this because it is important to know that I am not just involved in the rental home business. The participation in other real estate ventures along with my quest for further education keeps me well informed and knowledgeable in a wide variety of opportunities.

Although I dabble in alternative business models for a variety of reasons, I don't stray too far from my base business model. It has brought me stable revenue, financial security, and a comfortable life style I wouldn't trade for anything in the world.

. . . My simple business model . . . has brought me stable revenue, financial security, and a comfortable life style I wouldn't trade for anything in the world . . .

And Finally The Questions This Book Will Address . . .

The following are some of the key questions I have wrestled with as an investor that you will find described in this book:

Chapter 1
How do you capitalize on a pig in a poke?

Chapter 2
How do you know how far you should go in improving your property?

Chapter 3
Have you thought about what should you bring along with you when inspecting a property?

Chapter 4
What should you do when you see a dog?

Chapter 5
When is the best time to sell a property?

Chapter 6
What does a ticking time bomb look like?

Chapter 7
What will you do should your flip flop?

Chapter 8
What investment opportunities do you see here, if any?

Summary
When it's all said and done, what remains at the end of the day?

CHAPTER 1

Now That You've Got The House,
What Are You Going To Do About it?

There have been times when I have ended up with houses that I may not have been looking for. The purchase of the house pictured above is a prime example. My Father found this project for us when we needed one to keep all of our construction crews going. This house is located in a little higher end neighborhood than most of my other properties and I knew that it would take a couple of years for the house to break even. All of that considered I felt it was worth doing the project and it kept my operation going. At the time I had several other projects coming up and did not want to lose the crews that I had working. This philosophy hasn't always worked out well for me but this time it was ok. This house has been a fairly good rental for nine years and will continue to be good for my portfolio. It is just one example of the many ways I have ended up with properties. You may have similar experiences. For example, a rental property may have come with your primary residence. You inherited it or maybe it was just too good a deal to pass up. It doesn't matter how you acquired it, how you financed it or even what your ultimate goal is. You now have a house to deal with. So what are you going to do about it?

In This Chapter

However you acquire rental property, you will have to eventually make decisions and take action that will have an impact upon your financial fortunes. This chapter lays out a concept about how the very same decision-making and action opportunities faced by all property owners are viewed and taken advantage of by a very successful, professional real estate investor.

What To Do With Your First Rental Investment House

People acquire their first investment rental properties in a variety of ways – some intended, others unintended. Many folks start with their first investment rental unit when they rent out a spare room in their home or a room in a detached garage or "granny unit" in back of the main house. Other people become landlords of investment rental properties when they buy a second home to better suit their growing family and decide to keep their first home as a rental investment. In the case of the current economic conditions, there are some folks who have moved out to their new homes and have been unsuccessful in selling their original homes, forcing them to rent out the original homes because they can't afford to pay two mortgages. You might call this **"organic" acquisition**, as distinguished from straight acquisition when someone just decides to go out and purchase a rental property on the open market as an investment home, vacation home or retirement home. Still other folks find themselves with investment rental property when they inherit property through probate. Finally, others receive investment rental property as a package deal when part of the purchase of their primary residence includes a rental unit.

However you wind up with an investment rental house, at some point you ultimately will have to decide what to do with it. By this, I mean, you will have to determine:

1. to what "extent" to be involved in the investment rental "business";
2. how to assess the condition of your investment rental house;

3. whether or not to renovate the investment rental house in order to put it on the market either for sale or as a renovation;
4. how to manage the construction of the sale of the investment rental property renovation;
5. how to conduct the property management and property maintenance process as part of the rental business; and
6. when to sell.

It's in the knowledge, skill and experience in addressing these points that we have built our company fortunes to what they are today; for we are very clear about the business model that works best for us and very good at fulfilling, coordinating, and managing all of the steps to achieve our business objectives.

I think not enough people realize how much money they may be leaving on the table by not finding the right answers to these questions or finding the right talent that can assist them. So let's go over each of these points in more detail to see what I'm talking about:

1) Determining to What Extent to be Involved in the Investment Rental "Business"

Most owners of rental properties are part-time investors who spend very little time managing their investments and derive very little of their income from it. I know this to be true. I've seen the statistics on the demographics of landlords in America and Canada (see the American Housing Survey 2009 update that comes out every two years put out by the U.S. Census Bureau and the Canadian Mortgage and Housing Corporation (CMHC) on the 2005 report References page in the back of this book for specific citations). Most landlords own a small handful of investment properties that they are renting out. Over half of these landlords own 5 units or less; and moreover, over a third of them own 3 units or less. Less than 20% of all landlords derive their primary source of income from rental properties and up to 50% of landlords earn less than $20,000 per year from these rentals. Estimates show that there are approximately 15 million landlords in America. Over 90% of these landlords manage their properties by themselves.

. . . there are approximately 15 million landlords in America . . . (and) over 90% of American landlords manage their properties themselves . . .

Clearly although the majority of these landlords are participating in what may be technically called a "business" for tax purposes, they are not participating in what I would call "the full immersion serious money making business" of growing, developing, and managing real estate investment property. The question is, are the majority of real estate investors satisfied with having "just a toe in the investments waters?" Are they participating in their minimal way because:

a) they are bewildered about what to do next;
b) they are new to the business;
c) they are satisfied with what they have;
d) they believe they are financially constrained;
e) they don't know enough about the business to go further; or
f) some or all of the above?

My hunch is f) -- some or all of the above with a strong emphasis on a) that investors are either bewildered about what to do next with their property windfall, or e) investors don't know enough about the business to go further.

The focus of this book is to give existing investors, "wanna-be" investors, and potential investors direct answers to their questions about what is possible with investment in real estate as a business – something more than the minimum involvement business model that a majority of people are following for whatever reason. So to the questions of –**"Now that you've got the house, what are you going to do about it?"** and "… how to determine to what extent to be involved in the rental business?",

I say pay close attention when reading this book: See what's involved as an investor on a part-time basis as compared with a full-time basis; see alternate ways of being involved in the business from part-time to full-time; and see whether you can be comfortable being involved more-of-the-time or full-time. Whatever level you choose to be involved in is entirely up to you. You must recognize, however, that you have a business whether it is with one rental unit or 100 -- a business that can be very satisfying on all levels. The book and I are here to give you those options.

. . . The focus of this book is to see . . . what is possible with investment in (rental) real estate as . . . something more than a minimal involvement business . . .

• **What Is Real Estate Investment?** The term "real estate investment" can mean many different things to many different people. I want to expand your concept of what real estate investment means to me in this book, and **the first concept to grasp is – that there exists a full-time (or greater than part-time) real estate investment business model that works and works very well**.   As I've said before, I know this because I am engaged in it more or less full time and have been engaged in it since I was 12 years old.

• **What Is Full-Time Investment?** Let's talk about full-time investment for a moment here. The predominant concept of real estate investment and perhaps many other forms of investment is that it is an activity that is mainly passive – part-time. You the investor spends some time, usually part-time engaged in the investment activity from time to time – perhaps in research or oversight, but for the most part you are engaged full-time in something else that is not the investment activity – something that can range from full-time employment to full-time enjoyment or full-time retirement.   The "investor" image, is therefore a somewhat higher level or higher status occupation than most other forms of work (that require active, full attention engagement), implying that you have money to invest – money that is over and above what you need to survive on –

and that the money is what is doing some meaningful enabling "work" instead of you. In this popular notion, "investment" is work, one step removed from "real work" that requires real time hourly engagement.

The term "investment" is also tied in with the concept of money instead of time. People who spend time in pastimes of their choice are frequently thought of as volunteers, not investors; whereas people who spend "money" – itself a form of "bottled" time, on the same pastimes, are called investors.

Investment and real estate investment also implies a form of long-term attention to some form of "business" as distinguished from speculation. Investment and especially long-term investment is regarded as a higher form of engagement as distinguished from speculation, which is regarded as a short-term form of gambling.

Finally, in absolute terms, "long-term" investment technically means longer than a year according to the IRS. In real terms, long-term can mean anything longer than a few months.

Popular definitions of investment and long-term real estate investment don't necessarily fit with my understanding of these terms as I practice them:

- First of all, **I'm in real estate investment as a business** in the sense that I'm in it to earn a good living at it –a full-time living using a robust, seasoned, and sustainable business model.

- Second, **I'm in real estate investment for life** -- for the long-term -- way beyond three months or even one year. I've been in my version of the real estate rental business for 15 years already and I'm just getting warmed up!

- Third, **I'm "all in" the real estate investment business**. It is full-time in the sense that it is almost always on my mind or not far from being on my mind, even though I don't spend a lot of time at my office. I devote all of my professional energy to it. I've invested not only a lot of money that I have earned and put right back in to the business, but also a lot of time – much of which goes unaccounted for (meaning I don't watch it all that carefully. I just do what I find necessary to be done). All that being said, I still have a good, balanced life in and away from real estate. Have I mentioned that I am very happily married; have a beautiful family of five children; have a beautiful home; am an avid fisherman; and also have a charter boat business? I have a lot of friends whom I spend time with and there is a lot of laughter in my home. I believe that I have achieved a very happy balance in my life.

- Fourth, **I don't regard my real estate investment business as being on more than one level**. I am willing to do just about anything to further my business . . . from the meanest, to the most modest, to the most important of tasks. I will do whatever simple, ordinary, or ugly, boring, nasty task is necessary to keep it going in the right direction. I don't understand how people can look down on any part of it. I absolutely love what I do and every part of it.

- Fifth, **I rarely speculate or gamble with my rental portfolio**. I don't have to because I have many options open to me. Of course, I do speculate on other real estate investments and I increase my odds for success as much as possible. The logic of gambling on short-term profits with my bread and butter houses, however, works against me . . . for in taking short term profits, I am cutting off my chances for long term gains in appreciation, and tax advantages such as depreciation and more favorable capital gains tax rates. Perhaps in the next chapter you'll see what I mean when you go through the list of the many ways that are open to me to earn money on my real estate investments.

- Sixth, **I have a professional staff to handle all the key parts of my real estate investment business**. In this sense, I don't do this all myself as the ±90% of those involved in the real estate investment business do. I believe that we as people all have special skills and preferences that are different from each other. I also know that I have chosen and know very well what I like to do, what I'm good at, and the converse – what I don't like to do, and what I'm not good at. And like most people, I want to maximize the time I spend on what I like to do and am good at and minimize the time I spend on what I don't like to do and am not good at. This is a round-about way of saying that although I'm a practical person and know intuitively that it doesn't make sense to hire a lot of staff to do what can be done easily and efficiently by yourself, **I also know that it is foolhardy for me to do many things that need to be done in my business when I'm not the best suited for the job**. Since I have a long-term perspective about my business and a comfort level about the scale of business I wish to operate. I have chosen to build a great team around me that does the things I'm not very good at, nor don't very much know how to or care to know how to do.

People have told me with significant frequency to the point where I am a believer, that I'm very good at and enjoy working with and managing people. My peers also tell me that I'm also very good at the overall coordination of renovating homes. This is fortunate, because I enjoy both of these management functions. On the other hand, the same people tell me I'm not particularly good at finance, day to day property management, ongoing property maintenance, accounting, clerical, and a thousand other things that are done in my business (designing homes, painting houses, laying carpet, plumbing, electrical, and on and on) although I have a good understanding of what's involved in all of these necessary occupations. This too is a good thing, because I'm not particularly good at nor do I enjoy doing all of these other things, so I have found people to help me that are. And as my portfolio has grown, so has my staff to fit the scale of operation we have grown to be.

. . . People have told me with significant frequency to the point where I'm a believer that I'm very good at and enjoy working with and managing people. . .

Now perhaps you're thinking that you don't need a staff to help you if you have just one or two rental properties in your real estate investment portfolio, and you're probably right. But let me assure you that if you're going to get more serious about the business of running a real estate investment business, as in aggressively increasing your portfolio, then you need to begin seriously considering hiring a staff – someone other than yourself or your spouse. I have asked our chief operations officer, who has been with my organization practically from the beginning, what are the break points in terms of the number and kind of staff that you need for the scale of operations that you have, assuming that you start in to this business as a part-time person. You'll find her answer in Chapter Three. For now, know that my organization started with three people –our Chief of Operations Officer (COO), my Dad, and me. We all had different skills and interests. Our COO was an experienced property manager; Dad was and still is very good at acquisition and finance; and I was either very lucky or pretty good at managing people and renovations. Together we made a great team. We didn't begin the business totally without skills, as we all had been practicing our individual skills for years prior to our starting our company. On the other hand, we were new at building a comprehensive real estate investment business and had to obtain some on-the-job training in the process of finding our way.

. . . I don't do this all myself as the ±90% of those involved in the real estate investment business do . . .

I'm mentioning this because I'm suggesting that you may also need to follow a similar path to find your way. As we found out, there was nothing to fear here because we were armed with the attitude that whatever we couldn't or didn't want to do ourselves, we could find good people who would and could do things better than we could. . . and we were okay with that.

All this being said, determining to what extent to be involved in the rental business is key to knowing what to do with the investment real estate house, now that you have it. If you can see extending yourself beyond the rental of one or two properties into the world of robust business opportunities that exist if you follow in my footsteps, you may be surprised to find yourself richly rewarded someday. What you need first and foremost is the vision of the possibilities that this book is providing for you and the knowledge that you too can build a competent team to fulfill all the necessary functions needed to succeed at whatever scale of operations you are comfortable with.

2) Determining How to Assess the Condition of Your Investment Rental House

By now, you may be beginning to get the full, comprehensive picture about what, why, and how I do what I do. If you have been following my logic, then you also know that the core of what I do is centered around the process of acquiring, renovating, and managing the rental and maintenance of investment homes. **In short, it's all about the house.** All else flows from the house.

All of it begins with selecting the right house in the right neighborhood, in the right condition. So what is the right condition?

Well, I've already described for you the kind of neighborhood to look in (first time buyer) and the type of property to acquire (single family). I've also suggested that you look at a modest home – by which I mean under-designed for the neighborhood, smaller than normal, or in run-down condition – I call them the neighborhood "ugly ducklings". I've told you that purchasing this kind of property at below market pricing will give you the opportunity to spend some money on renovation upgrades to add value to the house that will enable you to be able to sell the house for a profit immediately upon completion of renovation, or more importantly rent the property out upon completion of renovation with positive cash flow . . . meaning the amount you are receiving in rent covers the carrying cost of the home (monthly mortgage + renovation costs + ongoing property management fees + annual maintenance costs).

This all means that if you've ended up with an investment home that is much fancier than what I've described here, I suggest that you sell or exchange that home and purchase or trade for another home matching the description above, remembering all along that this is business and because it's business, the numbers have to work out.

Once in the right kind of home in the right kind of neighborhood, you're ready to assess the condition of the investment rental house. To do that, you're going to need to **hire someone like me to consult with if you've never been involved in a renovation before**. Either that or you're going to have to acquire all the skills yourself by putting yourself through a multi-year apprenticeship similar to what I went through in which you become intimately familiar with the construction of the main elements of houses and all the trade specialties that contribute to it's development.

Selecting the right home to renovate for rental purposes is easy for me because I have acquired the right skills to make the assessment. Like a surgeon, I know what I'm looking at in terms of condition, costs, remaining life and rental home standards. Besides all of that, I just love doing it! I enjoy going through a house looking for the existing problems and exploring all the possibilities that others may or may not see. I don't purchase every home I look at even if many points of my criteria list are fulfilled. For example, **I don't buy homes that have been in a fire; I don't buy homes that are in scary neighborhoods where there are drug dealers; and I don't buy homes that I can't purchase for a low enough price to repair and create positive cash flow**. I look for homes I can make "landlord-and-resident-friendly", homes that standup to the normal activities and wear and tear of children, and homes that I can keep an eye on and afford to repair and manage despite the bad habits of some of my residents.

Are you getting my drift? After finding the right neighborhood and the right category of home to be investing in, assessing the condition of the investment rental property is the next most important step. Assessing the condition of the rental property is important because it is critical in determining what is possible in terms of renovation, how much to offer for the home, and how to manage the home once it becomes a rental property in your portfolio. Assessment is a job that can be done by a trained eye. If you do it well, you are well on your way to a happy career; and by this I mean you'll be able to be much more efficient at staying away from poor choices and selecting the few good choices in the sea of bad ones. This will save you time, energy, and money. You'll make fewer mistakes. Your company will do better and you will find yourself with a larger group of sustainable, money making properties that will be far easier to manage and less problematic in the long run. All of my staff knows well that we make our money on the buy, not the sell. While I'm not perfect in following my own advice, for the most part I've succeeded.

3) Determining Whether or Not to Renovate the Investment Rental House

Sometimes I get lucky and I find the right investment house that is in the right place, for the right price, and requires little to no renovation. Mostly I find these situations in my dreams. In reality, most homes require renovation in some manner even if it's just a new coat of paint and a few new toilets. Most homes that I find are several decades old and at minimum, many of the fixtures are obsolete. Other homes I find have overgrown or just too much landscaping that requires too much maintenance for a rental unit. Still other homes have obsolete rooms in the home that will never be used (formal dining rooms for example) because people just don't use them anymore in today's world. Roofs frequently require replacement. Old flooring material is often better off discarded. Electrical circuitry frequently requires updating as well as hot-water heaters, stoves and refrigerators. Bathrooms and kitchens usually need some updating. Sometimes there's nothing wrong with the house, but there is an opportunity to substantially increase the monthly rental by adding a bedroom or two. I can usually figure all of this out in few minutes on a quick tour.

There are periods of time when I've had to get several renovations underway every month for months on end. Believe me when I say that this is very demanding work. I only mention it because I want you to realize that in doing so, I've seen what I consider to be most everything you can see in terms of renovation issues, and yet I still learn something new everyday. All of this experience has made me good at this. I've made plenty of mistakes in the process, but by and large, I believe a major part of the success of my business has been the result of my correct assessments in this area – **making the right renovations for the right reasons at the right time.**

4) Determining How to Coordinate the Construction of the Investment Rental House Renovation

My primary skill, if I have any at all, is in managing people. I've mentioned this before. Oh, I can swing a hammer and put up some drywall in a pinch, but so can a lot of other people. Where I think I may excel is in the coordination of all the trades and steps of construction in the renovation process. To me this comes very easily. It just flows. Moreover, I really enjoy the process and I know what I'm doing. Others have told me how much they appreciate how well I do this job too as most of our jobs get completed on schedule and very smoothly.

. . My primary skill, if I have any at all, is in managing people . . .

If you're going to engage in a lot of renovation such as I'm suggesting that you do to build the kind of successful investment real estate rental business that I have, you will probably need to fill this role with someone like me. What many have told me makes me effective is that I combine many skills in one person: I have all the knowledge of all the trades that can participate in a renovation from plan preparation, to permit approvals, to site engineering and to house construction; I also have all the knowledge of the logistical scheduling of a foreman; I have all the intangible skills of enjoying people; and I have the street knowledge of knowing how to work with people so everybody wins, even in high-stress situations when things go wrong.

Like so many businesses, real estate investment is a people business. This is made more complex by it being a business full of many people who need to take many steps in coordination with one another. The plumber is only concerned with his plumbing; he is not worried with any of the steps that come before or after him, even though all these have to be coordinated. The roofer, electrician, dry wall installer, carpenter, painter, and carpet layer are all the same. Each and every tradesman involved has this uncompromising tendency to over focus. They also have the inclination to point the blame at each other and to not play nice together as a team. One of the key roles of the person in charge is that of peacekeeper and coach. When in this babysitting, handholding, and cheerleading role, I frequently use humor to lighten the mood as schmoozer-in-chief. When things have settled, and people have put their egos down to the point where they are ready to listen to reason, I present a resolution. Someone has to make sure that the job just gets done. It doesn't matter who is getting along with whom at the time. This is why you must have someone on your team that sees the big picture and knows how to fit all the pieces together harmoniously.

5) Determining How to Manage the Property Management and Property Maintenance Process

Once all the searching, screening, negotiation, acquisition and renovation are completed, we move into a long term phase of renting out the property to families, conducting cost effective property management and initiating long term maintenance. The trick here is to keep looking for ways to keep ongoing costs as low as possible. We do this by trying to be smart – minimizing outfitting and furnishings to eliminate as many things that need to be replaced from our investment homes as possible. We also try our best to save and conserve materials whenever we can. Another way we save is by trying to avoid being "penny-wise-and-pound-foolish". **We are always thinking long term, so if the only way we can do this is by spending more in the short run to enable greater long-term savings, then we proceed.** As I've described earlier, we buy at wholesale rates in bulk when we can. For example, we may purchase five refrigerators at a time if the opportunity comes up to save on them. We also invest in employee training (including for me) to keep our employees thinking about coming up with improvements in our operations whenever possible. Another thing we do is constantly drive through the neighborhoods and inspect the inside of homes to gather intelligence on our properties whenever we have the opportunity, so we can nip anything in the bud that doesn't appear to be going our way. For example a resident that is parking on the front lawn or has a broken window is typically not taking great care of the inside of the house.

Each house and multi-family complex has a unique set of circumstances as part of its internal make up. As soon as we possible can, we try to determine what those unique circumstances are in terms of what to expect for property management and maintenance. We then make adjustments to our overall procedures to try to make operating and maintenance more efficient over time.

6) Determining When to Sell Properties

I mentioned four options for selling property a few pages back. There are actually a few more:

- Sell immediately after renovation – something we rarely do
- Sell or exchange to rid ourselves of unanticipated low quality properties based on our internal scoring system or trading up to higher quality property (quality defined as stable, appreciating, low

operating and maintenance costs, with excellent residents) – this has happened a few times and will probably continue to happen over time

- Sell when one of our residents wants to buy the rental property they are living in – we have done this several times and it always ends up a win-win
- Sell when we need the money for one reason or another – this happens occasionally
- Sell when we've reached a high point in the recurring real estate appreciation cycle – this can be hard to predict, but we're ready for it
- Sell when one or more of the positive cash flow factors changes so that cash flow can no longer be cash flow positive – this is what happens when I over-leverage a particular property (for example, refinancing it to take equity out) -- not a good practice
- Forced to sell by government condemnation or unanticipated disaster such as fire – we haven't had this happen yet, but it could

We normally don't sell our property investments for any other reasons. We just hold on. Holding on has been and is good business for us.

Summing Up

You wound up with an investment rental property. Now what? This chapter has been all about how to turn this opportunity into a real business as I have. I've taken you through the statistics of what many investors do when faced with such an opportunity – nearly nothing. I maintain that they are leaving a lot of money on the table, largely by not understanding what they have or their options. The truth is that the investment rental business opportunity, although engaged in lightly by over 15 million Americans, has scarcely been scratched. Thus, opportunities abound.

I, on the other hand, have shown you how I've created and operated one of the best businesses on the planet . . . a business Warren Buffet may love to own with multiple income opportunities and nearly infinite flexibility to build a secure nest egg for you and your family no matter what skills you presently have. To get into this business, you first need to grasp the whole picture so that you can understand all that it entails. Once you've grasped this, you have a decision to make. . . whether and how to pick up the reigns and get busy. There are many ways to get involved in investment rental property as a business, but as far as I am concerned, few paths to building a long-term sustainable business with it. I've shown you one way . . . the path I've taken. Now it's your move.

CHAPTER 2

Providing Basic Shelter And A Secure Place To Live With The Investment House: Why Garbage Is My Life

Here is another house I just thought I couldn't lose on. The initial numbers looked great on paper and probably would have stayed that way, had I left well enough alone. But oh no, for some reason I let myself get too carried away with this project and am still paying for it today.

I purchased this house from a very nice French lady that had lived there for years. It was in my target market, in need of rehabilitation and at an asking price of just a little over $100,000, I was sure it would work. With the house in dire need of a new roof and a few other repairs in the unfinished attic, I was convinced that replacing that section with a full second story was a grand idea. I had been looking for a project to do this with for a while as I had several friends in other areas having good success with second story additions and wanted to give it a go.

The initial inspections and estimates with the architect and engineer went well and so we proceeded. At the time house prices were still on the rise and I let this add to my "how could I go wrong?" thought process. But let me tell you exactly how wrong I was. By the time the city was completed putting together their requirements, our little project had grown immensely. The structural requirements in the basement even caught my engineer by surprise. Looking back, this was the start of a "perfect storm" of investment development factors that ultimately sent this project over the brink and out of control. Complying with city requirements immediately cost us price overrun and time delay traumas, yet we pressed on. Hiring a series of incompetent contractors, one right after another added to our woes. Then, the one factor that I thought would be our saving grace in the face of mounting costs – rising home prices, all of a sudden leveled off as home sales started to slow. I was beginning to get the picture now that this may not turn out the way we intended, but thought we were way past the point of no return, so we had to complete what we had started. Unfortunately, by the time we had the project completed, home sales in the area were flat and we were in trouble. We had more than doubled our projected rehabilitation budget that made it unfeasible for us to keep the house as a rental. We were now counting on a quick sale in order to get out of it as soon as possible.

All in all, this was not looking good but we tried to sell anyway. This unsuccessful marketing period brought to light a few other mistakes I made on this project. First and foremost, I had broken one of my own rules about fitting in with the neighborhood by overbuilding for the area. The house was now bigger and nicer than any of those around it. In addition to that, I had not taken into account that this bigger house would have to have more parking than what had existed before. I had created a large 5-bedroom 3-bath home in an area that couldn't support it. What was I thinking? We currently have this home rented and owe more on it than we can sell it for. I forgot some of the things I had learned along the way and now have to hold on until we can get out of it.

In This Chapter

When investing in housing becomes anything other than providing basic shelter, trouble is usually right around the corner – a concept that is no longer what I would call investment. Unfortunately, we've just been through another round of this speculative fever that has disrupted all of our markets and turned our economic system on its head. I plead here for a return to sanity, knowing full well that this last round of insanity will make real estate investment even harder than it used to be.

Another Flip-It Flop – When the House Ceases to Become a Secure Place to Live

In the past few years, investing in real estate has been all about the quick flip using the greater fool theory – it's ok to bid the price of houses up defying gravity because there will always be a greater fool that will come along to bid it even higher and insure your road to riches. I've seen this so many times before, when the house ceases to become a secure place to live and becomes instead an inflatable toy to play games with. We never seem to learn the folly of this because "flipping it" seems to reoccur with regularity every decade or so. You can call it anything you like, but in the end, it's speculative gambling and everybody seems to get caught up in it. When everybody's doing it, it's a fool's paradise because when the music inevitably stops, many people get caught with no chair to sit down on, and they wind up "crashing and burning," to use a popular expression.

Flipping is not real estate investment as I understand and practice it. It is not real; it is not sustainable; and not sustainable is what I call FLIPPED OUT -- the title of this book. Flipping is not a business as I understand real estate investment to be. What else can you say about it except that it gives the kind of real estate investment I practice a bad name and makes it harder for guys like me to be in business, because when the crash comes, as it always does, the consequences mess everything up for the real investors.

What consequences? Well how about the new irreversible, permanent regulations which came down like a hammer making it harder to build, harder to get capital, and harder to purchase a place to live for individuals and families that have to live somewhere; or how about property tax assessments that rise when everyone is flipping houses and driving the value of homes sky-high, increasing the annual cost of owning homes dramatically, sometimes to the point of creating unfortunate foreclosures for those who can least afford it; or how about the rising cost of higher risk mortgages that increase monthly expenses and the risk of foreclosure.

. . . Flipping is not real estate investment as I understand and practice it. It is not real. It is not sustainable -- and not sustainable is what I call FLIPPED OUT -- the title of this book . . .

Who Wants To Be A Millionaire?

Who wants to be a millionaire? This was an interesting question even before the TV game show. Now the "get rich quick" guru's out there will have you believe they have some magical way for you to make huge amounts of money in your pajamas without ever breaking a sweat. These same gurus disgust me and insult the intelligence of real investors everywhere. Since you are this far into my little book, I will assume that you feel the same way. So let me be real clear on what I am talking about here. **Achieving success in real estate investment is work. This is hard work that at times is ugly, gross and disgusting.** On the other hand, what other business offers the rewards that real estate can deliver when it is done right? My business is awesome and worth all the blood, sweat and tears that I have invested. I can tell you that the real benefits are years in the making and well worth the wait. Becoming a millionaire in the kind of real estate investment I practice is a reachable achievement, but it will not happen overnight and not in your pajamas!

Providing Basic Housing Shelter for People to Live In

In it's simplest terms, being a housing provider the way I practice it is upgrading the existing housing stock. I go out and find housing that is old, out-of-date, run-down, broken-down, used-up, obsolete, ugly, ignored, and dysfunctional and turn it around so that it is the kind of housing that fulfills people's needs much better than it used to. Done correctly, what I provide is better than a lot of new housing that frequently has prices and standards that many people can't afford.

Another way of looking at it is I'm the house recycling guy who tears down the old, fixes, repairs, replaces, and renews all the broken parts and transforms the barely standing into a basic, safe, stable, reliable structure that people can build their lives around again.

Garbage is My Life

The way I engage in investment rental homes is as a business. It is not a sport; it's not a pastime; and it's not a second part-time job. I run my business using standard systems and procedures I've perfected over the years that work quite efficiently in providing a much-needed service. Shelter is one of the three fundamental human needs after all – the second leg of "food, shelter, and clothing". I've assembled a staff of experts who are very practiced at what they do in providing shelter -- that methodically transforms what many would call trash into treasure. This has been a wonderful business for me that I wouldn't trade for the world. This business has given me a privileged, secure, and happy life. On the other hand, as an activity, this business is not thrilling the way I imagine flipping it is to those who practice it. No one in my business has any illusions about becoming a "bazillionaire" overnight in one fell swoop. In fact, some of the time, what I do I occasionally have heard described as disgusting and boring. Real estate investment is not entirely the glamour job so many make it out to be. Ask yourself, what do you think of when you hear the words – "investment real estate"? Are you more likely to see sugarplums dancing in your head as a member of the privileged class or do you see disgusting and boring?

Garbage is my life is a metaphor that I've repeated to myself and about myself thousands of times over the last 15 years. It's the real view from the inside of the rental homes investment business looking out as distinguished from the fantasy view looking from the outside in. The vast majority of the time I am able to say garbage is my life with a smile on my face. And I smile because I am willing to do what others are not . . . that in the end, I will be in a position to reap many rewards. I would be hard pressed to think of another part of this business that separates me from the other "wanna-be" investors.

. . . Garbage is my life is a metaphor . . . (for) the real view from the inside of the rental homes investment business . . .

So now that you're here reading about it, would you like a real insiders view? Well, like it or not, garbage is a big part of having rental investment houses. In context, it's not as big as I'm making it out to be here, but it's one of many important things I do as part of this business.

Reality TV
Television is a very powerful and influential medium of communication and by in large provides good service in letting the public know what's available in the way of new goods and services. My beef with television gurus is that in trying to put the best foot forward about the products they sell, they don't get around to telling you the bad stuff. Romantic and sexy is the only sales approach they prefer using. Here is what I know from experience about my business. See what you think after visiting my reality show. Warning, some of the descriptions should only be read by mature adults:

- There always seems to be a pain in the butt, whiny resident that calls 20 times about the rodents in the attic but doesn't want us to hurt the poor little critters.
- Every once in a while we discover 5-gallon buckets that have been used as toilets in the bedrooms after the long eviction process
- "Normal" move out sometimes includes property damage that ranges from a few holes in the walls to every square inch of sheetrock in the house destroyed.
- Disagreements and collections seem to be never ending at times.
- Tons of garbage always magically appear on normal move outs.

- There is a massive amount of municipal paperwork and documentation needed to run a legal, upstanding business.
- Vacancy rates that are for the most part beyond our control greatly affect our bottom line.

These are not the things that make the TV shows and nobody ever wants to talk about them but they are real. These types of challenges show up from time to time and will happen to me again. I make sure I learn from every one of them but never let them get me down.

Take a look at just a small sample of what I deal with on an ongoing basis. This is reality. This is what having a real estate rental business is about. Now if you can smile at the end of these pictures and see the opportunities that are available when you are willing to do what others are not, than maybe you are right for this business.

GARBAGE IS MY LIFE

Here, in all of their glory are a few photos of life as I know it working with rentals.

Garbage is a part of this business whether you choose to haul it yourself like I do or to hire it done. Lets look closer at what I really mean by this. In case you haven't confronted this reality before, let me give you a tip -- rental residents will treat your house differently than they will a home of their own.

How will they treat it? The short answer is not well. Oh, there will be a few who are neat and clean no matter where they live, no matter what they own. But by in large, many renters live with a lot more garbage in and around their homes on a day-to-day basis than you're probably used to. You probably need to get used to the fact that under normal circumstances, renters will regularly leave a mess for you to clean up. No matter how well your renovation, maintenance and management systems are, these challenges will be there. This is the reality of this business. This is what I deal with every day.

. . . some of the time, what I do I occasionally have heard described as disgusting and boring . . .

The process of hauling and keeping up with the garbage of this business is one that I had to figure out and grow accustomed to over time. I started out by filling the dumpsters that were being dropped off onsite by the local hauling services around my area to clean up my renovation projects and other messes that occurred. After doing that for a while, I graduated to using a 6' x 10' dump trailer that I towed behind my pickup. Years later, I purchased a dumpster system that consists of three 8' x 12' dumpsters for my crew to use. As part of that crew, I deliver the dumpsters, then pick them up, dump them at the city dump and redeliver them wherever they are needed. This dumpster system was very expensive to initially acquire, but one that has paid off very well over time.

Hauling the garbage myself keeps me in touch with my crews and properties. This has become more and more important as my business has grown.

Summing Up

For me, real estate investing is all about providing basic housing for people to live in so that they can go about their lives feeling secure, stable and focused on the parts of life that are most important to them. I present the concept that "Its all about the house" as a my fundamental investment attitude – a concept that is entirely consistent about providing housing that fulfills the simple, fundamental shelter purpose for all humanity of having a roof over your head. I remind myself daily of the importance of this task by staying involved in hauling garbage. In my opinion, I must continue to like hauling garbage because this attitude keeps me closely in touch with my essential mission as a real estate investor – also known as a primary recycler/up-grader/restorer of run down housing to ordinary people. This is a noble profession – one that I wouldn't trade for all the tea in China. Real estate investing is all about providing basic housing for people to live in so that they can go about their lives feeling secure, stable and focused on the parts of life that are most important to them.

CHAPTER 3

Business Model Choices When Investing In Houses

This house is a 3 bedroom, 2-bath rambler (after renovations) in a great neighborhood (stable, well maintained and attractive) close to an Army and Air Force base. The neighborhood is on the outskirts of our target market. Homes here have average prices a little higher than what we specify in our company business model. Despite all of that, we felt this was an exception worth pursuing primarily because the home fit the criteria of being the classic "ugly duckling" of the neighborhood that could be upgraded at a price that would show positive cash flow after upgrading. In our property grading system, we would rate this one an "A" – meaning one we would like to acquire, rent out and hold on to for a long time.

The house was purchased at a foreclosure sale with the to-be-dispossessed-owner still living in it. I knew this before making an offer, but decided that I was willing to take a risk that his temporary occupation would not pose a problem for me in persuading him to leave in a timely manner.

I had contact with the gentleman right after acquiring the property. He seemed to understand that he needed to leave the premises immediately, but he asked for a little more time to get his belongings out of the house. I agreed to give him a couple of days, guessing that the more time he took in moving his things out, the less time and expense I would have in disposing of whatever remained.

I showed up at the house with a coworker on the morning after he was to be out. As a courtesy, we knocked on the door loudly announcing our presence. Receiving no response to our knocking, we entered what appeared to be a vacant house and started making our initial inspection. After a very brief time, while I was inspecting the kitchen/dining area and my coworker was inspecting the garage, the previous owner appeared out of one of the back bedrooms looking dazed and confused and started stomping towards me with clenched fists and fire in his eyes. He appeared so threatening that I raised my hammer in self defense and tried to appeal to his better nature that he calm down as he continued to come towards me as if to do me harm. Fortunately, when I had retreated as far as I could in the kitchen, my 6'-5" very large, strong and intimidating male coworker appeared from the garage with a pipe wrench raised above his head and came into full view of the gentleman, stopping him cold in his tracks. Coincidentally, the very surprised and flustered house guest of mine decided at this point that it would be a good time to start a more civilized conversation; and from that point on, things worked out, and I'm really glad they did.

The point of this story is that this "A" property that has never given me an ounce of trouble since that time, started out with an uncomfortable confrontation. Clearly I was prepared to deal with the situation. I didn't assume that being in an "A" property would be any safer than being in a lower rated property. I brought along items that could be used as weapons in a confrontation (I always carry something with me to protect myself such as a hammer, pipe wrench or large flashlight) and I brought along a very intimidating looking coworker that turned a one-on-one situation into a two-against-one situation with the odds stacked clearly in my favor as a witness. The question is are you prepared? You need to ask yourself this and other questions like it, if you are to succeed smoothly in this business. All of this brings me to a key question for you here, namely how do you expect to do business in this business?

In This Chapter

Knowing what sentiments, preferences and goals you have about investing in real estate will help you focus in on the details of how to run your real estate investment business successfully. Here I ask you many of the tough questions that need to be addressed to help you select a business model that will work for you.

What kind of investor are you?

Being a successful real estate investor is a function of having both the right personality characteristics to handle the requirements, stresses, and challenges of the job and the right business model structure to earn your keep. About having the right personality characteristics, ask yourself what kind of investor you are now and what kind of investor do you want to be in the future? You should not take these questions lightly. It is one thing to go outside your comfort zone now and then, but quite another to get into something that goes against your very being. The following are the personality characteristics options as I see them:

• Nervous Nellie?

Are you the "Nervous Nellie" type of investor -- the one that can't sleep at night worried about everything that could possibly go wrong in the world? If you know you are, then do yourself a favor right now. Put your money back under your mattress and go back to sleep. Don't get into this business! Why? There is a lot of the unexpected that occurs in this business. You have to learn to expect the unexpected in this business. Things do not go as planned. House closings – for both buying and selling, get delayed all the time for various reasons. Projects themselves have all kinds of hidden surprises hidden in them that are unknown in the beginning. All the different people that you will be dealing with bring along their own set of challenges and constant change. A key member of your team is out sick or on vacation and you must regroup immediately. I have gotten used to things not going as originally planned and not "counting my chickens before they are hatched." I have also witnessed a lot of people get out of this business because they just could not get used to it all.

. . There is a lot of the unexpected that occurs in this business . .

- **Suffers From "Analysis Paralysis?"**

Do you suffer from analysis paralysis?   Do you analyze every possible scenario to death twenty times especially for processes you've never been engaged in before?   Have you ever encountered the situation that when and if the time comes that you have made a decision, the deal has been long gone?   You will have to overcome this through experience. There will be some real growing pains and you will make mistakes. I make them everyday. The trick is to get in the game and do the best you can. Learn as you go and keep on going. It will get easier as you go and the mistakes will become less and less painful.

You have got to get yourself in the game in order to have a chance at winning.   I have spent a lot of time with new investors over the years and I enjoy it. For the most part they are excited about getting into this business and eager to learn. What I do not enjoy is when I discuss the same project with them for months on end and answer the same questions over and over again. I try to express the importance of making a decision and moving on but sometimes to no avail. Although this may disappoint me, I can appreciate their hesitation and try to help.

This business is not for the meek or uncertain type of personality. I recall the stories I have heard of the great generals that believed that their job was to make decisions. Right or wrong they made them, with or without all the necessary information available; then, without looking back, they made the next decision based on the next situation where there was only imperfect information available.

. . .This business is not for the meek or uncertain type of personality. . .

Timely decisions are an important aspect of this business and one that cannot be taken lightly. That being said, it is also important that these decisions be put into perspective. Lets look at my crew and me for example. It is a well-known fact that I not only want their input on our projects, but also encourage them to express both their ideas and concerns. These are discussed and taken into consideration with all others. I make the decision based on the information available and my experience and that is that. We all move forward from there until another decision is needed, which in this business will be very soon due to all the unknowns we deal with on a daily basis. There is no looking back. There is no finger pointing or placing blame when things don't go as originally planned. I shoulder all responsibility. This is the only way I can reap the benefits of having the people that work with me free to share their ideas. I also realize that I am an exception when it comes to how I work with my crew. I have been told over and over again how they feel more valued working with me than others. I enjoy working with my crew as a team and have been very successful with this approach. I am the general, but they are the most important.

. . . Timely decisions are an important aspect of this business and one that cannot be taken lightly . . .

- **Shoots From The Hip?**

Oh, I so wish I did not know this investor type for I am guilty of it many times over and I know how much trouble this causes. This is about as opposite as it gets from the analysis paralysis type. I have had the experience of getting a little cocky, thinking I could make any house in town work into my program without doing my due diligence and following my own system. Man does this hurt! I have been in situations where I have done more guesswork than homework and I can tell you that it has cost me. I have a few unfortunate houses that I know I should not have gotten involved in and would not have gotten involved in had I stuck with my program. Sometimes, shooting from the hip can be more dangerous than just staying home.

... I have been in situations where I have done more guesswork than homework and I can tell you that it has cost me ...

- **Rainy Day Ronny?**

How does that old saying go? Expect the best but plan for the worst? In this business it is not if things will go wrong, it is just a matter of when. When I say wrong, I do not mean catastrophic; just not as planned -- the wall that I was just going to paint now has to be completely torn down and rebuilt; the sewer system is all of a sudden inoperable; and the same house seems to have eviction after eviction for reasons I can't explain. The list goes on and on. The unexpected is a part of my everyday life. I have adapted a philosophy that enables me to smile my way through it, however. I suggest you do the same.

... Expect the best but plan for the worst ..

- **The Pushover?**

Do you buy anything the stockbroker calls about so as not to hurt her feelings? Is the one experience you had with a rental memorable as a disaster because you couldn't bring yourself to evict the tenant from hell you had? Are you too meek to negotiate with a strong personality to get a good deal? If this is you, then you need to put things in a little different light. Let me help you with this. Think of non-eviction as taking food off of your family's table, because it is! When you have rentals, it needs to be profitable, as in a business, or it's not possible to continue doing it, right? If you have a problem with this, you probably shouldn't be in this business. On the other hand, maybe you just haven't learned how to show people you are negotiating with how they can win in your deal, while at the same time enabling yourself to say no to things that don't work for you.

. . . *it needs to be profitable, as in a business, or it's not possible to continue doing it . . .*

I can be nice and still do good business. I handle this quite often by stating the fact that it is about business. Behind in rent, not keeping up their end of the deal -- whatever the case may be can be handled both nicely and professionally. I can't call my mortgage holder and tell them my resident is having challenges. They do not care. The way I handle this is to stay polite but professionally take care of the situation. I smile and shake hands with the folks that owe me money just like I do with the others. Most of the time things are not personal here. Just business.

Residents that are having challenges paying their rent can be helped in other ways besides just foregoing the rent. I have helped some of them move to less expensive homes that I have or worked out a more favorable payment plan for them. If they are honest and respectful to me, I will do what I can to work with them. It is always my intention for things to work for everyone involved not just my business.

• **Nerves Of Steel?**
Do you have nerves of steel? Are you the type of investor that "has been there, done that"? Be careful not to bite off more than you can chew especially in the beginning. If you take on too much and can't manage it right, it will cost you. It makes a lot more sense to grow this business deliberately and with a plan.

I have been a little of all of these at times over the years. I would describe my style of investing as being very aggressive, almost to a fault. I enjoy having a lot going on. When we were heavy in the growth phase of our portfolio, I had several crews and subcontractors going at the same time. This was a little crazy, almost overwhelming at times, but a lot of fun. It was more than a full time job just to keep ahead of the crews.

I have had a tendency to take on houses with some real challenges and have learned from all of them. Some of my "brilliant" ideas I had at the beginning of the projects did not work out so well so I adjusted along the way.

. . . Be careful not to bite off more than you can chew . . .

I have worked hard to hold true to my business criteria and have been pretty successful at it. I have been very good at not getting emotionally attached to any house or particular idea. I just want what works.

I place a very high value on education – always trying to learn as much as I can along the way either from the school of hard knocks, or from classes, seminars and books.

It has been important to me from the very beginning that I run my business with the long term in mind. I've tried my best to avoid being like so many "flash in the pan" hot shots in real estate who ride high during one economic cycle only to then crash and burn later on when they can't sustain the business models they are following, such as what has recently been called "flipping".

What Are Your Investment Capabilities?

Think about what your investment capabilities are right now. Make sure you are looking at things realistically. There are many ways to get where you want to go in this business. I know this to be true because I have used a lot of them. This is not a one size fits all business. The following are factors to consider:

- **Lots Of Cash And Free Cash Flow?**

If you have cash and good cash flow, you have many options. Cash is king, as the saying goes and it is definitely true in real estate. Having a lot of cash, however, doesn't mean that the most prudent thing to do is to pay "all cash" for properties as they become available.

Leveraging your cash into many more properties over time than what you can simply purchase with all cash or with highly restrictive financing terms is what has made real estate such a superior investment vehicle to all other forms of investment. For example, if property you've acquired doesn't qualify for conventional financing, you can use your cash leverage to rehabilitate, then refinance this property in a manner that will enable you to create and maintain a positive cash flow while it is rented. . . minimizing your risk and maximizing your leverage. This is one way that worked well for me.

If you have a lot of cash and cash flow available, the most prudent thing to do is to keep as much of this cash available as you can to spend on opportunities that inevitably will come up and rainy day problems such as unexpected or routine maintenance or market downturns that are also inevitable. As I just described, I try to leverage cash carefully on a short term basis to acquire property, rehabilitate it, refinance it – working the numbers carefully so that I can transform the property into existing on a self-sustaining basis – carrying the expenses of owning it all by itself in a situation I call positive cash flow.

. . . keep as much of this cash available as you can to spend on opportunities that inevitably will come up and rainy day problems such as unexpected or routine maintenance or market downturns that are also inevitable . . .

I make it a point not to get myself into a situation where I am overleveraged – which I define as being unable to do what having a lot of cash enables. How much cash is enough cash to do this? There is no fixed number. It's a judgment call influenced by a variety of factors. My advice to myself is to be as conservative as possible with cash guarding against "the perfect storm" that can and probably will happen somewhere along the line, when I can least afford it. I accomplish this by asking myself a few "what if" questions that have a high likelihood of happening. What if I had to replace 5 refrigerators in one week? Would I have the cash? What if property stopped appreciating? Could I sell the property and still be okay? What if my vacancy rate tripled? Could I carry the mortgages by writing checks for a number of months until new qualified renters could be found? Okay you get the idea. Available cash is the least costly, best form of insurance against the unlikely, but eventually inevitable circumstances that life presents us with.

- **Lots Of Access To Credit?**

Do you have access to substantial credit? Access to substantial credit is almost as good as cash, but it's more expensive. Credit is not free. It costs money that cash doesn't and can be very expensive in a variety of economic conditions. In any case, it can be used in the same way as cash to leverage ownership of a lot more property value then can be paid for at the time of purchase. Having substantial credit will enable you to build your portfolio fairly fast. . . if you use it prudently – cautiously and conservatively. Here again, you will have to make sure that your long-term holds (houses you are planning on keeping as rentals) are financed in such a way that they at least carry themselves. Having houses that have a negative cash flow when they are rented out doesn't work for me because I am forced to use up cash reserves, then after my cash is used up, more expensive credit reserves to carry the property. This doesn't work because it is unsustainable -- if I keep doing this, eventually I will use up all my reserves. As with cash, one good use of substantial credit is to take advantage of unexpected and unforeseen opportunities as well as a hedge against non-routine, low probability "rainy day" or "perfect storm" problems -- both of which are inevitable at some level. Credit used this way is a form of affordable self-insurance. It's a lot cheaper than purchasing insurance.

. . . Credit . . . is a form of affordable self-insurance . . .

• How Long Can You Wait Things Out (Short Term Vs. Long Term)?

Give some good thought to your timelines. How long can you carry a project before it develops a positive cash flow? How many projects can you financially handle at one time? How many simultaneous vacancies can you self-finance? Things do not happen at the speed of light in this business. There are a lot of variables in each and every project that take much more time than you will want. You, as the investor, are really the only one that time matters to. Your cost of funds (interest, fees and opportunity costs) can eat up any potential profit or equity really fast. The interest clock on borrowed funds ticks away every day and you will be paying for that. Believe me, the jurisdiction that is delaying your permit or inspection does not care how long your project takes. The contractor that shows up a week later than he promised doesn't care either. You are the one that it affects. You have to plan on some delays during the projects and then just work as hard as you can to minimize them. Having planned for some extra time with the funds to handle it, will save you a lot of frustration and stress in the end.

. . How many projects can you financially handle at one time?. . .

• Little Cash, Little Credit?

If you have little cash and little credit don't worry. There is a place for you in this great game of real estate. The acquisitions may be a little harder to come by and things will happen a little slower than you would like, but you can get started now. Dig in and learn as much as you can. At this stage it is more important than ever to make sure you are building on a solid foundation. You can't afford to make big mistakes. Remember, people will always be selling houses. Some of these may be more than willing to work with someone they believe in. This can be you.

What Are You Investing For?

There are many reasons to invest your hard earned money. You need to define what your reasons are. There could be one big one or several things that you want to accomplish along the way. Ask yourself the "why" of what you are doing this for. There will be many a day in this long journey that you will question your decision to get involved in this business and you need to have a viable reason for doing it.

• Appreciation?

Appreciation has been oversold as of late. Just look at all the "flippers" that have got stuck in this economic meltdown we are all currently experiencing. Betting on appreciation to continue on a never-ending road should not be your only exit strategy. Appreciation is an added benefit -- not an investment strategy.

. . . Appreciation is an added benefit – not an investment strategy . . .

• Tax Benefits (Depreciation, Deferral)?

Talk to your tax consultant to determine what benefits you will see from investing in rental homes. My accountant is an integral part of my team. I include him on overall strategy discussions at a minimum. Do I buy more properties now or wait? Am I in a position to sell a few properties this year or do I wait till next year? Having your accountant involved in more than just doing your taxes is vital to your success. The information that he can provide you along the way can make a huge difference to your bottom line.

. . . Having your accountant involved in more than just doing your taxes is vital to your success . . .

• Steady Income – Positive Cash Flow?

Positive cash flow is awesome! I want my entire portfolio of rentals to have positive cash flow overall. During the course of the year, several homes will need roofs, have vacancies and evictions. All of these will affect the cash flow of my company. I have to have enough other homes with positive cash flow to make up for this shortfall. When you start out with the first few rentals, this is particularly difficult to achieve. Think about it. When you have four rentals total and you have one vacancy, you have lost 25% of your revenue. It is pretty hard to have the other 3 make up that difference. You still have to strive for it. Getting involved in properties that increase your rental value right away will enable you to accomplish your overall positive cash flow goal a lot sooner. Positive cash flow should always be the goal.

• A Specific Need?

I have a good friend that purchased his rental houses when his kids were young and planned on selling them to help pay for their college. He found good deals and his plan worked out pretty well. Even the last one that he sold when the market was dropping was of great benefit to him due to the fact that he bought it long ago when he perceived the need to do so. Do you have a specific need in the future you can start funding now? When you have the kind of clarity that specific needs can provide, it can be a remarkable vehicle.

. . . the kind of clarity that specific needs can provide . . . can be a remarkable vehicle . . .

• Filling A Market Need?

Have you found a need in the market that needs filling? For example, is there a college that is expanding and needs more housing, or is there a new industry that will increase the demand for housing in your area?

Study market needs very carefully. Make sure it is an actual need that you can capitalize on and not just mere speculation.

. . . Make sure it is an actual need that you can capitalize on . . .

- ### Speculation (Leverage)?

Speculation is gambling. I have nothing against it, but you have to understand what it is. I have developed land and built new homes on speculation, but it does not play a part of my rental business. I do not buy more properties in the areas that are being restored (as in urban renewal) or changing for other reasons than I do anywhere else. Just because the local newspaper says some area is the up and coming place to invest in doesn't make it so. I have seen many guys lose their shirts while waiting for these types of changes to occur. Be very careful about speculating. Make sure it makes sense with or without the expected changes.

. . . Be very careful about speculating . . .

- ### Why Did I Invest?

My rental portfolio was built for the long haul so I have rarely used my accumulating real estate investment profits to fund short term needs. In line with this philosophy, I have always tried to provide for my immediate family requirements through engagement in other business ventures so I could leave my real estate portfolio untouched. This explains why I adopted a policy of having my rental houses pay for themselves while rented.

For the most part, this approach has worked well. As my real estate investments have continued to perform well with the systems that I put in place, I have been able to keep growing the investment. Throughout the entire process, appreciating asset value has been an added bonus, but I have never counted on it. The use of tax benefits from these investments to offset other income we have earned, has really helped over the years as well.

. . . My rental portfolio was built for the long haul . . .

What Kind of Investment Vehicle is Attractive and Suits You?

Once you have decided to invest in the rental housing business, there are many different avenues you can take to get started. You may find, as I would suggest, venturing into a couple of different investment vehicles to create some diversity in your investment portfolio. You don't want to have all of your eggs in one basket, so to speak.

• Buy New, Take Tax Benefits, Wait For Appreciation?

Buying new homes for investments is a tough way to go. First of all, forget about going for the fluky deals – i.e., it's just not possible to purchase a home in a new development when it is 30% complete and sell it upon completion of the project for a huge profit. This method was always an anomaly, if and when it was possible anyway. There may be other gimmicks new home developers come up with to tempt you with from time to time. My advice is to tread lightly and look carefully before you leap. Unless you are very experienced in real estate matters, you could be burned badly. Take it from someone who has been there.

Second, one of the principal advantages of investing in new homes as rentals is the newness of the homes because like buying a new car, there is little if any maintenance cost to be concerned about for a significant time. On the other hand, because of the high acquisition cost of a new home, it is usually very hard to make the numbers work. Positive cash flow is darn near impossible in the beginning.

Third, the other main advantage of investing in a new home is having a house that is fashionably trendy – the kind of house that delivers high pride of ownership. The principal advantage here is ease of renting as trendiness is nearly always in high demand.

> *. . . because of the high acquisition cost of a new home, it is usually very hard to make the numbers work . . .*

I know investors that built their units themselves using this kind of approach and have done fairly well over the years, but they went into it with their eyes open and knew what they were doing. They used their building and development skills to keep their building costs as low as possible and prepared themselves for the risky business of having negative cash flow for a time – even a long time. These guys took this approach to meet their own high quality standards telling me that they wouldn't rent anything that they would not live in themselves. Now, I'm not saying this approach should not be taken, but it does limit the available options by making it much more difficult to financially succeed.

• Buy An Existing House At Market Value, Take Tax Benefits, Then Wait for Appreciation?

Looking to purchase the same homes that everyone else is looking at poses a couple of challenges. For one, these are the homes that most shoppers are looking at to buy for themselves. Now a shopper that is emotionally involved in the purchase of a house to make it his or her own personal home, raise kids, and have Christmas dinner with his or her family, may pay more for it than an investor will. Thus a buyer intent on living in the home will have a distinct competitive advantage over an investor.

> *. . . a buyer intent on living in the home will have a distinct competitive advantage over an investor . . .*

This is not a good position to be in as an investor. Now, I have purchased a couple of properties in this category along the way and in both cases was able to make the economics work due to seeing something no one else saw: a way to drastically increase the house's rental income and value, that made it possible to create positive cash flow. Finding additional bedrooms within the structure is one way I have been successful at making the numbers work in this situation. This is one of the key reasons that I try to avoid buying in this market. It's just too hard. Now you might ask, aren't all homes subject to this situation – aren't all homes being looked at by people who will become emotionally attached to it as a home to live in? Perhaps this is true. I would say, it just seems to be more the case in higher end, up-scale communities than the communities I invest in.

• Buy An Existing House Low, Make Superficial Improvements, Sell (Flip It)?

Ah, the famous "cosmetic fixer" that every get rich guru wants to tell you about. These are fantastic when you can find them. Years ago it was a little easier to come across -- these simple clean up, paint and flip houses. I was having success with this approach way before it was as popular as it is now to do so. Before all the TV shows, sensationalism and outrageous increase in values we recently experienced, sellers were actually surprised to know that I would buy their house as is. They were grateful not to have to put all the spit and polish on it themselves and were able to move on. I was able to provide them with a real benefit that they previously did not know existed. These types of projects are still out there, but they are a lot harder to find. Along with their increase in popularity, came higher purchase prices. As soon as the masses showed interest in these projects, the prices started to climb. This was continually fed with the flood of media attention and cheap money. As long as the money was easy to come by, the inexperienced investors just kept bidding higher. This feeding frenzy was bound to come to an end sometime and boy has it ever.

. . . These type of projects are still out there, but they are a lot harder to find . . .

On the other side of this equation is the "flip it" part. As many people are painfully aware of now, this business model has some real risks associated with it. People don't always make money on a flip like some will have you believe. In the midst of purchase prices charging up, prices sometimes start falling like a rock, freezing the market (because no one buys once prices start plummeting) that, in turn leaves many who bought at high prices holding on to houses they can't sell and are worth less than they paid for them.

Thus having the sale of the house as your only exit strategy is not a good plan. As I have shown, the main problem is if the market goes south while you're holding on to it, you go down with it. Values on houses can come down as we have currently seen. I have done the fix and flip model many times, but always had other options available – long-term rental, to be precise. The fact that I've only been able to get the sale price I've wanted on flips in a timely manner about 50% of the time before being forced to put the flip in our rental pool (because the carrying cost has been too high) has increasingly discouraged me from participating in flipping. It only takes one of these units to not sell or sit empty for a bit to greatly drag down my whole portfolio. Knowing this risk really puts the brakes on my flipping except in the most ideal of circumstances.

... It only takes one of these units to not sell or sit empty for a bit to greatly drag down my whole portfolio ...

- **Buy An Existing House Low, Make Major Improvements, Then Sell (Flip It)?**

The houses that need more of a major rehabilitation to make them marketable have a little less competition for them principally because they cannot be purchased with conventional financing. What I mean is that to successfully negotiate the purchase, I will have to put together some combination of cash, lines of credit, and seller participation; and after making all of those tricky arrangements, I will then have to put together the financing for the major rehabilitation itself.

This brings us to challenge number two -- the actual work of renovation. These types of projects can easily go way over budgeted expense and time on their way to getting completely out of control for the inexperienced. Heck, these things happen to those of us that have a ton of experience. Unforeseen construction problems, personnel or contractor issues can be magnified in a big project like this. Make sure you are in a position to take something like this on before you jump into it.

• Buying Foreclosures To Get a Bargain?

Buying foreclosures is not for the weak kneed, scared of shadows investor. Foreclosures can be an enormous amount of work to do right. There easily may be more risk associated with them than you can safely estimate and let's not forget that ALL CASH is a requirement of purchase!

Now I know that in today's market, foreclosure-buying programs are getting very popular and things are changing everyday. In my experience with a couple of dozen purchases this way, risky is the best way of describing what can happen. I've had good success with the majority of my foreclosure experiences, but I have also made some blunders. Because an extra amount of due diligence is not only prudent, but absolutely necessary, look out for the situation where all you can do is drive by or walk around the outside of the house you are planning on bidding on, because the unknown may surprise you. The three-bedroom, 2 bathroom house that you thought you bought may turn out to be a 2-bedroom, 1 bathroom house with an unfinished attic. Ouch!

Once I thought I bought one house only to find out too late that it was really the house off the alley behind it that I purchased! I also made a $35,000 mistake buying what was represented as a first mortgage that turned out to be a second mortgage behind a huge first. That experience really hurt. What I'm saying is that even for experienced, well-healed investors that truly know the market, the foreclosure game may be risky, so tread very lightly in this arena.

. . . even for experienced, well-healed investors that truly know the market, the foreclosure game may be risky . . .

• **Buy An Existing House Low, Make Major Improvements, Rent, Sell?**
Eureka! The magic formula to success in the rental home business! I finally describe the one approach that I know works beyond a shadow of a doubt. I have done it many times and I still do it when I want to. It's reliable; it's low risk; and it's the formula that has worked for me time and time again -- buying the less desirable houses that need major improvements and lend themselves to ways of increasing rental revenue.

. . . I finally describe the one approach that I know works beyond a shadow of a doubt . . .

Being able to find more bedrooms within the structure has always been a great way for me to increase rental revenue and thus the overall long-term value of the home. In my market, every additional bedroom increases my rent by at least ±$100 a month (between $54-$217 depending upon the number of bedrooms). Done right, my renovation will look like it was originally designed to be there, probably because when I make the upgrade, I also modernize the interior layout of these homes by updating the kitchens and baths.

In the growth of our business, as it became more popular in our marketplace to buy and fix up older houses, I had to take on more challenging projects -- ones that the other investors were not qualified to tackle, such as ones where major structural repairs were needed. So although I have always wanted to do simple "cosmetic fixers", our desire to grow at a faster rate made it necessary for me to acquire more renovation skills to keep our growth momentum going. Acquiring the skills necessary to go after this model was challenging to say the least. Reflecting on this, there are not many investors that have my skills and experience or that of my team to handle this higher level of challenge. Not to worry though. If you find that you need to do what I did to effectively compete or grow rapidly in your market, I can probably get you there in a lot less time than it took me!

. . . If you find that you need to do what I did to effectively compete or grow rapidly in your market, I can probably get you there in a lot less time than it took me . . .

Where Do You Invest?

I have always thought that the location you invest in is as important as what type of properties you choose, following the tired but still true real estate mantra that the most important three things you need to know in successful real estate investment are "location, location and location."

The location that I have chosen to build my rental home business in is not unique to my town. There are areas like this anywhere and everywhere you go. It's kind of the middle of the road, ordinary working person's housing neighborhood. It's not the "romantic/elite" area where all the young, urban, upwardly mobile professionals (yuppies) are attracted to; nor is it the "scary slums" with crack houses galore, protective bars on all the windows and doors, and nighttime warzone helicopter floodlights and gunshots ringing out into the night. It is the working person's area in the middle. John Burley described this area very well in a seminar I attended. He said if you are driving the neighborhood and you notice that everyone is jogging in fancy jogging suits, it's too high end; and if you are driving the neighborhood and everyone is running like they are eluding someone, then that area is too scary.

. . . The location that I have chosen to build my rental home business in . . . is kind of the middle of the road, ordinary working person's housing neighborhood . . .

I hope you get the picture here. My area fits none of these descriptions. My area is for working men and women; or lunch pail John and Jane Doe; or blue/pink collar whatever you want to call it. I am not trying to be politically incorrect here. Rather, I'm attempting to describe the area that I know works for my kind of real estate investment. In the areas I invest in, we have young families with children, single, working women with children, and families of small business owners. Many people here are not in the professional classes. Most are wage earners, who go to work for a living in nearby businesses.

My particular area is in an older part of town where the majority of the houses were built in the early 1900's. The City of Tacoma, Washington has been described as a mid-sized, urban port city. It has been characterized as one of the easiest cities to walk in as well as one of the most stressed out in the last decade (Wikipedia, on the internet). Go figure? With a population right around 200,000 and median income of just under $50,000 per year, Tacoma is roughly 30 miles Southwest of Seattle and 30 miles Northeast of Olympia – the capital city of the State of Washington. It's an ideal bedroom community serving both of those areas.

The Port of Tacoma is located in Puget Sound and has been growing to meet the import/export needs of the State of Washington. In recent times, it has been providing a steadily growing supply of local jobs.

You probably have the John and Jane Doe "lunch pail area" near where you live. It may look a little different geographically and the houses may be a little newer, older or of a different style, but you probably have the ideal area right under your nose in your community that will work well for single family rental investment. Study your local community closely and choose wisely.

What Kind of House Do You Want To Buy?

You have to put some thought into what kind of houses you want to invest in and their condition. Are you in this business strictly for the monetary advantages or does pride of ownership hold an important position with you? How much time and effort are you willing to put into these houses? Two of the five models described below will show you what I have used successfully to build my rental home business:

• A House You Personally Would Like To Live In

O.K. look, if you think for one minute that your investment houses are going to be anything like the house that you personally live in, then you need to reconsider your entire investment strategy. Reality is that emotions may be what have you in the house you live in now. Although you may not be living in your ultimate dream house, I know that you and/ or your significant other saw where your furniture would be and colors you would want. You picked out the curtains, wallpaper, and decided the yard was just the right size. You made an emotional attachment early on, maybe even the moment you pulled in the driveway. This emotional attachment has no place in the selection of your investment houses. This is strictly a business in which the financial returns have to be right and work to your advantage. What's more, you are not going to be living there, so why does the home have to look like you would want it to, if you were to live there?

. . . emotional attachment has no place in the selection of your investment houses . . .

O.K. so maybe, you've now decided get into the real estate investment business by renting out, what you formerly lived in? Unless the numbers work, my suggestion is that you sell this house and find another to rent out where the numbers work out better.

- **Above Average House For The Neighborhood**

The nicest house on the block is not one that you will typically be able to buy and turn into a financial success. Don't get me wrong. I definitely want nice houses around – especially ones that I own or have my investment homes in close proximity to. On the other hand, I just know that I'm not out to purchase it as a rental home investment. Why? Because my financial flexibility as an investor is too limited when I buy the nicest house on the block. I probably will have little to no room for making money because chances are the home will be selling for top dollar. Dad taught me the first principle of making money is buying low and selling high. Buying the nicest home will probably not be buying low.

In addition, the primary prospective buyer for the house that is already all dolled up and looking good is someone looking for a home to live in. This may be too much competition for you to be able to buy it at a low enough price. Always remember you have maximum flexibility to make money when you make your money on the buy!

- **Average House For The Neighborhood**

When you sense that you are looking over the average house in the neighborhood, you are getting closer to what you eventually want to wind up with. Actually this is close to what you will want when you finish renovating, but you don't want it as an investment product to purchase. You want to end up with the average house but you may not be able to buy it right off the bat. You most likely will have to work for it in order to be the owner of the house for the right amount of money. On occasion, I have purchased houses that did not need any work and were purchased for the right amount of money, but I have to tell you that they are kind of boring. Its ok, I know that I'm a sick man!

. . . You want to end up with the average house but you may not be able to buy it right off the bat . . .

• Below Average House For The Neighborhood

Now that we are at the below average house, I'm getting a little more excited. This is the house that has some real possibilities for increasing value immediately. This is what you are looking for -- to make your money right away. So if the numbers work, buy this one; rip out the carpeting, update the house, clean everything up and bring it up to the standard of the average house for the neighborhood. Though it may not be the deal of the century, you will have a lot better chance of the numbers working to achieve a positive cash flow in this model than in any of the previously discussed houses.

• A House Way Below Average For The Neighborhood?

The house that is way below standard can have even greater opportunity for increasing value than the house that is just below average. This more challenging project comes with greater risks and takes much more time and effort than any of the houses in better shape. This extra time translates into additional risk -- a risk that should not be taken lightly. A severely run down, well below standard house is a different animal right from the start.

. . . The house that is way below standard can have even greater opportunity for increasing value than the house that is just below average . . .

As it is in this run down condition, conventional financing for the acquisition of the house is out of the question. The good news is that this financing limitation makes it more difficult for your competition to buy it. You, on the other hand, will have access to cash or maybe some seller financing to get into the house. Then you will need more cash for the major refurbishing and refinancing when it is renovated and pretty again. Do you see how all this is going to work?

One of the biggest challenges, besides whatever specific problems there are with the house itself, is time. It will take twice as long to do the first few major renovations as you think. Once you gain more experience, perhaps only one out of four will take too long. Time is your worst enemy and you are the only one that will intensely care about it. The contractors and public jurisdictions are not the ones with the interest payments clock ticking. Time is eroding away the good deal you worked so hard to get into. I have built a successful business by buying these types of houses, but I have also made my fair share of mistakes in trying to rehabilitate them. I've had to learn the hard way what I can fix and what I can't. I also have learned the hard way what is worth fixing and what projects I need to walk away from. This type of project requires this kind of experience and level of expertise. If you don't have someone competent to successfully maneuver in this area, don't get involved in this type of house.

. . . I have built a successful business by buying these types of houses . . .

It's All About Making the Right Choice

Life is all about choices. Investing is no exception to this. There are lots of choices out there that may or may not work for you. The devil is in the details and sometimes in the subtleties. You have to make the choice that best fits you, your family, your lifestyle and your goals. Look around, explore a little and get some education before you get heavily invested. The following are important considerations about choices:

• About The Investment Model That Fits You Financially, Psychologically, And Fulfills Your Goals
When looking for the investment model that will fit your needs best, be sure to consider several of the following basic ones:
- What investment model has the highest likelihood of meeting your financial goals? For example:

- Is the best model one that includes new construction homes that will more than likely have negative cash flow for many years, but will have a higher probability of lower maintenance and possibly higher resale value in the future?
- Is the best model the middle of the road rehabilitation that can be closer to financially carrying itself (i.e., having positive cash flow) right from the beginning?
- Are you planning on cashing these houses in at some time in the future, say to finance a college education or supplement your retirement or are you going to leave them to your heirs intact?
- How do you feel about being a "landlord" including performing all of the duties that it entails, as I've tried to describe them to you?
- When your buddies call you a "slumlord" are you going to laugh or cringe?

You need to think about all of these before you get started and position yourself accordingly.

• The Models That Give You The Least Choice

Some of the investment models I've described leave you with few choices as far as exit strategies go. If your only option is to sell right after you purchase and provide superficial upgrades, then what will you do if the house doesn't sell right away?

Short term financing and an unforeseen hiccup in the market can destroy all hopes of coming out ahead. I don't think I'm being overly pessimistic in reminding you of this. The market does not have to fall out of the sky for this to happen. It just has to move far enough to inflict significant damage to your investment expectations. I have had times when the local news media has reported that a large, local employer may possibly experience layoffs sometime in the future, which in turn resulted in potential buyers for my properties getting cold feet and withdrawing their offers. I'm not talking about facts here, just reported speculation. I want to note that nothing ever happened. The speculation was just enough to make news; the news, in turn, was just enough to make my buyers nervous; and the buyers inaction was just enough to make me sick when three of them pulled out. My point is that it does not take much for the market to react in a way you don't want, and when it does you can get caught up in it for a while.

. . . it does not take much for the market to react in a way you don't want . . .

Another model that may not leave you with many choices is when you own rental properties in an area with very low demand and slow sales. The overall model may be good for cash flow if it works to perfection, but if you are unable to get out when you want to, it can really limit your options.

Circumstances change all the time and for this reason investment models that give you the fewest choices are the least desirable to me. I want lots of options available all the time, but that's just me. How about you?

. . . investment models that give you the fewest choices are the least desirable to me . . .

• The Models That Give You The Most Choice
The models that give you the most choices are the ones that require rehabilitation, renovation or refurbishment. Using them properly will give you three options right away: 1) You can fix and sell (flip) now; 2) You can fix, hold and rent out with the rent covering the underlying payment; and 3) You can fix, hold, rent out and sell sometime in the future. The more properties you have with all three of these choices, the more diversified your portfolio will be. Over the past 15 years, I have grown to appreciate having all of these options available. Let's look at these choices in more detail:

. . . The models that give you the most choices are the ones that require fixing, renovation, rehabilitation, or refurbishment . . .

• Fix And Flip Right Now

If you take this approach, you must understand and accept the risks -- the biggest one being that the market may take a dip and you may be left with a house that you can't sell that is worth less than what you've invested in it. It can even get worse than that when the market falls off the cliff – far and fast, as we have just experienced. The cost of holding on can have just as huge an impact on your finances as the cost of letting go.

The fix and flip model can work and has worked well for me at times in the past. It works the best when you have more than just the immediate sale as an option as to what to do with the house after purchase. I always go into a purchase knowing about these additional options. I buy the house, fix it up and put it on the market for a limited time. If that time expires without a sale, it goes into the rental pool where hopefully, it immediately gets into a revenue generating capacity. This is how it works. I know going into the project that the numbers will work either way. I have not overextended myself purchasing the house without being able to take out long term financing; and I'm not stuck paying for a house that I have for sale in a down market for months on end.

• Fix, Hold and Rent Out With The Rent Covering The Underlying Payments

Will the rent cover the underlying payments (mortgage, property management, maintenance, insurance, taxes and repairs) when a resident occupies it? This is a must for me. I have to look at long term financing options at the time and make sure it will work. I also have to look at how much a property will cost in payments and operating expenses over time. Different people have a different impact on elements of the house. Resident turnover happens; weather impacts happen; tax laws change; recessions occur; accidents happen; and parts of the house wear out non-uniformly. All of these things need to be considered as possibly happening throughout the holding period; and of course, the longer the holding period, the greater will be the likelihood that any or all of these things may happen.

• Fix, Hold, Rent Out And Sell Sometime In The Future

Now I realize that no one knows what will happen in the future to the market or the world for that matter, but I need to be comfortable about the home's future value in order to fix, hold, rent out and sell sometime in the indefinite future. The home needs to be in a settled area (preferably filled with working, stable families, not declining, and not scary -- filled with drug addicts or gangs); the home needs to fit in (not be overbuilt, nor the ugliest home in the neighborhood) with the rest of the neighborhood when it has been fixed up; and it needs to look like a house someone will be proud to call home (in a good location, modernized (not obsolete), attractive, clean, having features people will find attractive and functional). Sometimes it takes a while for all of these features to materialize. For example, sometimes neighborhoods improve and sometimes they decline over time.

. . . The home needs to be in a settled area (preferably filled with working, stable families, not declining, and not scary . . .

How Much Money Should You Invest In Real Estate?

This is a both a business model as well as a personal preference question. Whatever kind of question it is for you, it may all come down to five choices: 1) Invest a little (0-10 Units); 2) Invest a moderate, balanced portfolio amount as a part time job (11-20 Units); 3) Invest as a full time job for one person (21-40 Units); 4) Invest a significant amount as a major part of your investment portfolio (41-75 Units); or 5) Go all in with more than a handful of employees (76 Units and Up).

This question, that is harder than it looks to answer, was never really decided for me until after it was done. Let me explain. Real Estate Investment as in purchasing houses and renting them out for a living, as distinguished from investing in the stock market, the art of old masters, or stamps, for me was never a question. I grew up with real estate. I've worked in it one way or another since I was 10 years old. The question was not whether I would be involved, but how, and how much.

This road that I took to get where I am today has been interesting as well as educational -- education being one of the keys along the way. Buying into my father's theory of non-stop continuing education was the best thing I could have ever done. The hundreds of hours and many thousands of dollars invested in real estate seminars, self help seminars, and business and personal coaching, has paid off many times over. For example, having first hand experience with many of the real estate gurus over the years has been very valuable. I didn't always agree with their real estate advice or teaching methods, and I strongly disagreed with the numerous ones that paraded real estate around as a "get rich quick" scheme. Regardless, more often than not, I learned a little something from each of them and this is the attitude I went into each seminar with. I was there to pick up on those one or two little things that would help my business. I found that I was not one that would follow just one teacher, nor did I ever suggest that to anyone else. I needed to learn from all of them. I was at a free mini seminar that blew into town a few years ago -- you know the kind that send you the free tickets and then get you in the door to up-sell the heck out of you with stuff from guys you never heard of, but have a great way of getting the crowd all excited. Well, I was in attendance for a short while (all I could stand) and ran into a gentleman that I knew there. He was baffled at my presence and asked what in the world I was doing there. My response seemed to bewilder him even more. I explained that it was important for me to know what others were going to be doing in my town even if I didn't agree with their tactics. I told him that I felt doing this usually gives me a leg up on the competition when I know more about what their trying to do than they do. This explanation made good sense to me, but I don't think he stopped shaking his head long enough to hear it.

. . . Buying into my father's theory of non-stop continuing education, was the best thing I could have ever done . . .

Continuing education has also contributed to the twists and turns my path has taken along the way. Having learned both new construction and remodeling at a young age allowed me to work using both bodies of knowledge later on. The skill of combining the two approaches I have found to be rare amongst the contractors I've known over the years, but one that I possess. So as I was getting beat up more often than I cared to while building new first-time-buyer-homes (the endless fussy demands of the buyers, the failed sales, and the neighbors upset when you build in their area) the discussions I was involved in about building a rental business around existing homes excited me. Granted the work needed to remodel a 60 year old house is far from glamorous, but it was exciting to me just the same. My team (all 3 of us at the time) figured we would buy and fix a few run down houses, turn them into homes, then live happily ever after. O.K. I might be oversimplifying a bit there, but you get the idea. As near as I can recall, we planned for about 20 homes at first. Unbelievably, that modest beginning grew to 50 homes a few years later and more than 100 a few years after that, giving us a machine that I didn't want to stop. It sure is strange how that happened. Through this entire rapid growth phase, I also had other projects going on to help support the rental business that was being built. It was a crazy time indeed that spanned over a decade. Many a days ended with me saying "someday I am going to be really glad I did all of this."

Now as I look back on how this happened, it's kind of all a blur. We wound up investing what to most people will probably appear to be a significant amount. We went all in, so to speak and I 'm glad we did. I'm not sure how much further we will go at this point, because I need to clarify my business and personal goals in order to proceed.

However, should I decide to continue, I have an excellent platform from which to proceed.

What I would like to go over now are the different business models you might consider as far as "amount of investment" is concerned and would like to say something in retrospect about what these general approaches entail. Before I do, however, I would like to say there is no easy answer to the question of how many is the "right number" of units to invest in. A 10-unit apartment building in relatively good shape normally takes ½ the effort to manage as 10 single-family homes in relatively good shape. Why? The 10 apartments are normally very similar to each other, and are confined in one area, so advertising (signs, ads, flyers all aimed at a specific customer) and maintenance are the same thing times 10. Each single-family home is usually very different from each other, so you need to have 10 marketing plans and have 10 different roofs, exterior upkeep, plumbing, and heating, to maintain. The location is also an important factor, 10 units in a highly desirable area are easier to keep rented then 10 units in a not so desirable area (even rentals go by the location, location, location mantra). Thus, the numbers given below are simply done on the average of having ½ apartments and ½ single family homes in average condition in an average neighborhood.

. . . there is no easy answer to the question of how many is the "right number" of units to invest in . . .

O.K. so now have I got your head in the right frame of mind yet? Are you starting to understand that there's more to the question of how many houses you invest in than meets the eye? Good. So with that, let me ask this question another way. How many of the "right" houses will it take to meet your goals? Yes, I'm trying to give you a hint that it is helpful to ask the "how many" question together with the question of what you are trying to accomplish.

Owning rental houses is not near as glamorous as it may seem. Although I can teach you the best houses to get and all the systems to put in place to make your life easier, it is still work -- work that I love but work nonetheless. When thinking about your potential numbers consider how many people you may need on your team to make it work (financial staff, renovation staff, maintenance staff, property management staff, office, cash, credit lines, office space, maintenance equipment) needed for different numbers of units. I did not do all of this by myself. I couldn't have.

The number of houses you have rented out and your growth rate are directly related to the amount of talented people you need on your team. Building a successful team in this business is a chapter in itself and one for later discussions. Here I want to just have you thinking about what you will need at the different levels. You can manage 1 to 6 houses with one rehabilitation project going at a time. At this level you are still at your full time job and taking care of your houses in the evenings and weekends. Not to worry though. Your kids will really love spending their Saturdays mowing lawns and hauling garbage. They just don't know how to show it! This is a very sensible approach and you will be involved in each phase enough to learn what works and what doesn't. This learning is very important especially when you decide to move on to the next level.

. . . The number of houses you have rented out and your growth rate are directly related to the amount of talented people you need on your team . . .

If you decide not to have a team because you're a go-it-alone kind of rough individualist, not good at managing others, or not convinced that having others will help you be more productive, then you need to carefully consider how many units you can manage by yourself while working a full time job. Let's look at that same example again to see how feasible going it alone may be: A 10-unit apartment building in relatively good shape probably takes half the effort to manage as 10 single-family homes in relatively good shape. Why? The 10 apartments are normally very similar to each other, and are confined in one area, so advertising (signs, ads, flyers… all aimed at a specific customer) and maintenance are the same thing times 10.

Single family homes are very different from one another, especially in older neighborhoods, so you need to have 10 marketing plans and have 10 different roofs, 10 different exteriors to maintain, 10 different plumbing schemes, 10 different heating systems, on so on and so forth to maintain.   Location is also an important factor: 10 units in a highly desirable area are easier to keep rented then 10 units in a not so desirable area (even rentals go by the location, location, location mantra).   Thus the numbers shown in the work estimates below are made on the basis of an average of averages -- having half apartments and half single family homes in average condition in average neighborhoods.

- **Invest A Little (0-10 Units)**

0-10 units = A single person with a full time job should be able to manage and still have a life.

- You should have a handy man available. Even if you do maintenance yourself, sooner or later something WILL happen when you are not available (sick, vacation, at work…)

- **Invest A Moderate, Balanced Portfolio Amount As A Part Time Job (11-20 Units)**

11-20 Units = Someone with a part time job, you will be busiest the 1st & last week of the month:

- Rents tend to be paid with maintenance requests.
- Most lease signing and move in inspections happen from the 28th – 3rd of month
- Move out inspections usually happen between 28th – 1st (don't forget to do the deposit reconciliations within the state guide time lines)

- Definitely will want a handy man available for maintenance and to do rental preps to insure quick move-outs and move-ins. People looking to move normally need to give their landlord 20 days written notice, so you want to insure your available units are ready and advertised as much before the 10th of the month as possible.
- Carpet cleaners and house cleaners are good to know.
- Roofer, electrician and plumber appear in your permanent Rolodex file.

• Invest As A Full Time Job For One Person (21-40 Units)
21-40 Units = Full time job
- First and last week will be busy with the items mentioned above
- Bookkeeping requirements will take up to a week to comply with.
- Need to keep up to date on landlord-tenant law to lessen chances of a lawsuit.
- Handyman suddenly becomes a permanent fixture on your budget, or, you are seriously considering hiring a part time employee.
- The carpet cleaner, house cleaner, roofer, electrician and plumber are on your speed dial.
- Rest of your month is spent inspecting units, checking the subs work and paying bills.

• Invest A Significant Amount With A Couple Of Employees (41-75 units)
41-75 units = Full time job PLUS you'll want a full time maintenance technician and at least a part time office assistant to answer the phones (best thing you will ever do for your mental health is to personally quit answering the phones) and take appointments.
- At this point you really need an office for customers & residents to be able to come to for: Paying Rent, filling out applications, signing leases, requesting forms, etc... You may be able to get away with only being open the first and last week of each month. You will want a drop box.

- The maintenance technician should be able to handle most maintenance problems as well as paint, mow, and haul trash (trash begins to take on a life of its own about now). If you are thinking about saving $$ by hiring one person to do the maintenance, lawn, hauling, answer phones, show units... GOOD LUCK. In my experience, this has a low probability of success. The personality of most hands-on, maintenance-oriented people isn't consistent with the pleasant, professional image you want prospective customers and residents to see and still feel comfortable about renting from you. It's possible you'll find someone, but not likely.
- You should have at least a part time bookkeeper.
- You should have high-grade property management software to track leases, rent payments, resident charges, and deposits... We use a computer program named Property Boss.
- A website for advertising your available units would be justified.
- All your forms (leases, lead disclosures, pet addendums, move in-out forms...) should be personalized and on your computer (and regularly checked by an attorney to insure they meet all your state rental requirements). Realtors (with the perfect investor property for sale) call you daily.

• All In With More Than A Handful Of Employees (76 Units And Up)

76 and up = You are now a full fledged "real estate addict".

- You need a full time office, receptionist and bookkeeper. The bookkeeper should be able to cover the phones and front desk when the receptionist needs to go on appointments.
- You should have 2-3 full time maintenance employees.
- You are buying dump trailers, commercial grade lawn equipment and plumbing snakes.
- You may be teetering on needing a warehouse to house the above and to store materials you are now buying in bulk to save money.
- You ask your staff to include pictures of the house on reports (so you can remember which place they are talking about).

You should have a good computer program for scheduling and reminding you of yearly inspections, maintenance tasks (need to clean certain roofs every year because of trees, pump out septic tanks, have chimneys inspected…) and other bad to forget about items.

Summing Up

I have run a very successful real estate investment business using the strategic business model described in this chapter that gives me an incredible number of ways to benefit in the short and long term. With this business model, I've been able to flexibly work with normally fluctuating real estate cycles so that I minimize risk and maximize taking advantage of business opportunities. You can use part of my model or some of my model. However you decide to start, build or run your real estate investment business, know that I wound up doing everything described in this chapter, because I discovered through experience that it provided the best of all options.

. . . know that I wound up doing everything described in this chapter, because I discovered through experience that it provided the best of all options . . .

CHAPTER 4

Renovation For Different Investment Objectives

This house was an absolute dog when purchased for $57,000 in late 1999. I remember very clearly how much I liked it because it was very clear to me how much opportunity for improvement there was in what I saw. This was the classic undervalued "homeliest house on the block"—the kind of house I dreamt of finding that I could add tremendous value to through renovations. When I found it, the exterior had needed a coat of paint for the last decade; the main level of the house had little, if any remaining charm left; and what once must have been an appealing home in this part of town had been run down to the point of near extinction to where no family I could trust to treat it well would want it. The lack of maintenance was so obvious the moment I walked in that it immediately put a smile on my face. And as I toured the house, my spirits just kept on soaring. The hardwood floors had deep scratches; the kitchen was so much in shambles as to be nearly unrecognizable; and the basement appeared to have been the victim of several aborted, amateurish attempts at improvement. As I peered through the windows at the neighboring houses, my smile just kept growing because it became very clear to me that I was standing in the one house of all those in the neighborhood that really needed me -- the one that had the greatest potential for a huge immediate increase in value. At the end of my tour I thought, this one house, more than almost any other I have seen represented the kind of opportunity I wanted to pursue. This was exactly the kind of renovation opportunity that perfectly fit my business model. And with that, this run down ugly duckling was about to get a major makeover.

The complete rehabilitation included: finishing the basement with an additional bath, adding two bedrooms and a recreation room, updating of the kitchen, upgrading of the main bathroom and bringing the rest of the house into the 21st century with new dry wall, fresh paint, modern electrical outlets, and new carpet. When completed, this 5 bedroom, 2-bath home was worth far more than the $97,000 I had put into it. Actually, although I didn't realize it at the time, its value to me was even greater for with these improvements I was able to get a stable, long term resident that has rented this home ever since I restored it and currently pays $1,000 a month.

This incredible increase in value was created by the renovation process that has given me so many more options than it once had both then and now.

In This Chapter
Of all the steps you may choose to pursue in real estate investment, renovation is probably the most significant. Done properly, renovation (rehabilitation, refurbishment, restoration all describe a more or less similar process) will establish a profit base in real estate from which all other profit will flow and be enhanced. I describe here the key issues in renovation that enable it to be such an important factor in a sustainable real estate investment model.

What To Buy?
OK. First of all I have to tell you that the buy is the absolute most fun thing I do. I love to buy houses. The whole process is almost like a drug

to me: There's the thrill of the search; this is followed by the negotiation that everyone involved feels good about in the end; then there's figuring out a plan of action for the rehabilitation; and finally, there's putting everything into place. This is a blast. It's all good.

To specifically figure what to buy is best summed up fairly easily: Buy what makes sense for you and your market. And exactly what is that? Well, first of all you have to be comfortable with what it is you are getting into. It's not worth setting yourself up for sleepless nights over an investment property you hated from the very beginning. Your market will make your good and bad investments very clear to you over time. I will tell you that the investments that start out bad have a tendency to stay that way until you make more of a drastic change.

. . . investments that start out bad have a tendency to stay that way . . .

• Obsolete Floor Plan

I actually seek out these kinds of floor plans because they offer me an opportunity to make money. I've purchased many houses with obsolete floor plans over the years and have been able to increase value immediately by updating. In changing the flow and feel of the interior of the house, it becomes more user friendly. For example, many older homes in my area were built with numerous small rooms and not much thought given to the size or location of the bathroom or bathrooms.

• Just Plain Ugly

Ugly is the best deal going in my book. Ugly usually translates into deferred maintenance and therefore one heck of an opportunity to turn things around – overgrown landscaping, exterior peeling paint, and windows boarded up. The "ugly duckling" of the neighborhood is actually what I look for.

. . . Ugly usually translates into deferred maintenance and therefore one heck of an opportunity to turn things around . . .

• What if The House is Too Small?

Smaller houses are an opportunity as long as I can find more room somewhere to reorganize the space. For example, if it is for sale as a 2-bedroom but has 1,200 square feet of total living space, I will take a look and see what possibilities there are for additional bedrooms. If it's a 2-bedroom with just 850 square feet, I already know there is no easy way to increase the number of bedrooms within the existing structure.

What Not to Buy?

Don't buy houses or their sellers based on emotions. A lot of houses that I look at will not work as an investment for many different reasons. Some of the sellers that I meet with, I will not be able to help. I wish them well and move on.

Don't buy houses that have no opportunity for an immediate increase in value through renovation.

Don't buy houses that don't fit in with your overall business and investment plan (everything I've been describing in this book). This is another good reason to have your investment strategy worked out well ahead of time.

And whatever you do, don't buy houses that will not be self-sustaining after renovation -- cash flow positive with the rent covering the mortgage, insurance, and all operating and maintenance expenses.

. . . And whatever you do, don't buy houses that will not be self-sustaining after renovation . . .

What to Invest in, in the Investment House – Fixing, Enhancing, Adding, and Subtracting

When first looking at the house, I usually assess the damages that need to be repaired along with the opportunities for increasing value. This assessment will guide me through the renovation process. All safety items will get taken care of first. Then I will spend time and money on the items that will give me the most long-term value. Any repairs I make will be with the outlook that I will own the house for a long period of time and I don't want to have to redo repairs. I will go the extra mile in the initial rehabilitation to assure that everything is set up for easy long-term maintenance. This is especially essential in the kitchen and bathrooms.

. . . I will spend time and money on the items that will give me the most long-term value . . .

How Much Do I Spend on Renovation?

I spend as little as I can to accomplish my goals in the house. I establish a budget in the beginning of the project and then work as hard as I can to come in under it. As I've been describing, these goals frequently include adding revenue producing bedrooms and updated floor plans, eliminating the obsolete features, improving the appearance, adding safety features, and adding or subtracting items in order to lower operating and maintenance costs in the long run – hot tubs, free standing fireplaces, Koi ponds.

Who Should You Find to Help You?

Who is out there to help you? ME! This is a lot better than I had it. I had to figure out most of this stuff the hard way – with little or no help.

. . . Who is out there to help you? ME! . . .

What Should You Avoid?

I avoid properties that are on steep slopes, have previously suffered fire damage, are in the wetlands, and do not fit into my program.

. . . I avoid properties that are on steep slopes, have previously suffered fire damage and do not fit into my program . . .

What Not to do? – Intentional Destruction

I do not buy houses that need to be torn down. Now I have purchased several houses that the seller and realtors may have thought needed to be torn down.   The funny thing is that these homes still have my residents living in them; and as far as I can tell, these residents are enjoying them just fine.   Many people think that ugly and obsolete should be torn down instead of renovated.   I don't mind that at all.   These are the opportunities I live for.

. . . Many people think that ugly and obsolete should be torn down instead of renovated. I don't mind that at all. These are the opportunities I live for . . .

Summing Up

Intelligent renovation is one of the most important pillars of my real estate investment success. What I mean by intelligent renovation is I won't automatically renovate, just because I bought an old house. For example, if a 40 year-old kitchen is in good working order, I'll leave it alone.   Renovation, on the other hand, is a serious consideration and practice in every house I purchase.   It updates and upgrades obsolete houses; it increases sales (capitalization) and rent value; it lowers operating and maintenance costs in the long term; it facilitates appreciation; it enables taking advantage of the tax advantages of holding property; and it sometimes eliminates or resolves issues that arise in daily living for the resident and landlord alike. Renovation is so important that I recommend having a renovation specialist integral to your investment team on your team . . . a role that is so important to our team that I personally handle it. To perform the role properly, **your renovation specialized team member must know everything about how homes are constructed and are supposed to sustain themselves over time.** How important do you think that makes renovation to running a successful real estate investment business? In a word -- very.

. . . Renovation . . . is a key element in every house I purchase . . .

CHAPTER 5

Rental To Maximize Your Options: Property Management, Property Maintenance And Residents

I've owned this house for 11 years. It was in complete shambles when purchased and required a lot of initial work just to keep it from falling down. My oldest daughter was about 8 years old and was with me as I walked through with my crew early on in the project. When we got back into the truck she said she had something figured out. "Daddy, if the underneath of the house is ok and the roof isn't too bad, you can fix everything else, right?" Of course I agreed with her, noting that she obviously had been paying more attention over the years than I thought.

In having to put a lot of money into the structural and safety challenges of the house, I could not financially justify completing the update that I wanted to. Given its desirable location however, just a half a block off of a main arterial, I was ok with not doing everything I wanted to at once. I knew that our prospective residents would not expect everything shiny and new.

Years later I had to give it more of an overall update along with tearing down the old garage and building a new one. Thus, I found it necessary to remodel it twice. After the second remodel, a funny thing happened. The new resident inquired to see if we would sell it. He ran the oil change service station next door and wanted to be closer to his work – a move that would be better for him, his family and the neighborhood. While I had no plans of selling this house, it was easy to get to the decision to sell to him because I had already had 11 years of rental income, tax depreciation and value appreciation – more than enough benefits to recoup my purchase and renovation expenses and make a reasonable profit.

Taking the far view, the neighborhood (where we also have many more rental homes) was also ready to have another owner occupant who would make all those prideful little touches that make a house a home – a family that would create greater stability in the neighborhood and a win-win for everyone concerned. Who better to own this house than the people involved with the business next door? So in this case the best time to sell was best determined by the resident instead of me.

In This Chapter

Holding on to property long enough through renting to be able to maximize my profitability options is the key to my real estate investment success; and holding on to property through renting means mastering the landlord role. Are you ready for this?

What Is A Good Landlord?

A good landlord is one that you would like to know and deal with. This is a person that is firm, fair, and very clear about his or her policies. In addition, since renting is very much a people business, a good landlord is a "people person." This is a person who enjoys people and knows how to work with, through, and around any and all challenges smoothly and effectively so that everyone walks away a winner.

• The Mindset Of A Landlord

My mindset is one of patience and flexibility. I have to be this way. Having over 100 residents brings with it a wide array of challenges from routine to full of twists and turns. It's my role to be calm and decisive as the leader of my team. I also sprinkle in some humor in to keep the spirits high. I couple this with a persistence will to always do the best that I can.

• The Lifestyle Of A Passive or Active Landlord

I am a full-fledged "real estate investor addict", yet you wouldn't know it to meet me. I've spent the majority of my years in the back of the room, so to speak. In fact, up until this publication I have never told more than a handful of people the number of properties I have put together, manage or own. I live modestly and work hard every day. My princess and I have 5 teenagers between us and she has a full time job as well. I pay my taxes, drive Chevrolet's and vote in every election. Now you may have a life like me or you may not, but here are your choices as I see them. You can choose to do real estate investment:

- As a hobby – 1-10 units
- As a part time job – 11-20 units
- As a full time job -- 21-40 units
- As a profession -- 42-75 units or
- As a full fledged addict -- 76+ units

(see Chapter 4, for more description)

. . . I am a full-fledged "real estate investor addict". . .

I'm at the full-fledged addict end of the scale, and yet I have a pretty uncomplicated, enjoyable and balanced life. In other words, I don't think you should assume that a hobbyist has an easier, richer, fuller life selecting real estate investment as a hobby. No. I wouldn't assume that at all. In many ways, my life has become easier and easier the more units I've come to own.

. . . In many ways, my life has become easier and easier the more units I've come to own . . .

- **The Qualifications Of A Landlord**

As a successful property owner, I must comfortably wear many hats throughout the day, mixing many talents while maintaining a patient and fun loving demeanor. This is how I have chosen to build and keep my team running.

- **Financial Savvy**

I have had the distinct advantage of having the services of a father whose expert financial skills guide our business. His business savvy and banking skills have been instrumental to sustaining our growth and continued success.

- **Observational And Learning Savvy**

I observe and learn from everything. I have learned to continually sharpen my skills in many different areas. I attend everything from home and remodeling shows to real estate and construction seminars all over the country. I am always puzzled why people are surprised to hear about my attending these functions, but I think it is important to keep up–to–date in my industry. Besides this, learning is a lot of fun.

- **Construction Savvy**

My construction savvy is very unique in that I have an enormous amount of experience in many fields. This experience enables me to tackle a wide range of projects. I wish I could say that they always turned out as I expected, but I can't.

- **People Savvy**

I attribute a lot of my people skills to working on charter fishing boats when I was very young. Everyday in the summer, I had 20 different people on the boat for 10 hours and I was working for tips! I learned a lot about people from those experiences and it continues to benefit me. Having the ability to deal with people from all walks life is a big part of running this business successfully.

. . . Having the ability to deal with people from all walks life is a big part of running this business successfully . . .

- **Resourcefulness Savvy**

I am resourceful by nature and this has helped me in this business. I do not accept the first "no" that I get; nor do I give up when I confront challenges. People have learned to know this about me. Consequently, I'm usually counted on to know what to do when no one else does. I believe that being both resourceful and having solid relationships with people in my industry have enabled me to accomplish a large part of what I have achieved.

. . . I believe that being both resourceful and having solid relationships with people in my industry have enabled me to accomplish a large part of what I have achieved . . .

- **Flexibility Savvy**

I have learned that I must be flexible to maintain some sort of sanity in my life. I start out the day with an overall game plan of a couple of meetings and a list, but more frequently than not, all must be tossed aside based on what kind of calls came into the office. The resident that has a major challenge takes precedence over most, if not all of my other plans. I've found that I must adjust and maintain my flexibility with a smile on my face.

. . . The resident that has a major challenge takes precedence over most, if not all of my other plans . . .

- **Patience And Fortitude Savvy**

I have had to learn patience in this business. The fortitude to keep plodding ahead has come easier. Over the years I have joked that I just don't know how to quit. The truth is that I love what I do. I always have; and that's what keeps me going.

- **Willingness To Do Whatever It Takes**

I was taught at an early age that to be in any kind of business, I must be willing to do whatever is necessary to make it a success. I have structured this into my organization by example, not merely through by my words. Every person involved here knows that I am available to do whatever is needed at any time.

. . . Every person involved here knows that I am available to do whatever is needed at any time . . .

- **Management Savvy**

Management savvy comes over time and with a lot of education along the way. I have made numerous mistakes over the years that I work very hard at improving upon.

- **Building A Team Through Relationships**

Successful relationships are what building a successful business is all about. The ups and downs and the challenges that come your way are all manageable with good, solid relationships. My business thrives due, in large part, to the relationships that I have built and continue to build on a daily basis.

. . . My business thrives due, in large part, to the relationships that I have built and continue to build on a daily basis . . .

• My Team

My team started with the core people of my father, an experienced property manager and myself. This same core, our three-legged stool is still in place. Our philosophy, team concept if you will, has always been a division of responsibilities based on our individual talents. This team concept is still evident in my organization today. It is high priority to have the right people doing the right things. This in addition to establishing and maintaining the systems necessary to run a successful business is what has kept us sane through all these years.

While thinking about the concept of people on the team having different talents and responsibilities it is easy to look at what happens when this is not the case. I have seen this many times. Two house framers get together and form a framing company. Individually they are good framers. They both have the same talents. Together they are still good framers but may not have the other skills necessary to have a thriving business. Estimating, billing, accounting, human resource skills, etc… By this example you can see that one of the same framers partnering up with someone that possess' some of these other business talents may have been a better decision.

• Keeping On Top Of Things

I have to be in touch with what is going on in my business and the market around me at all times. I've learned the hard way that the times that I have been complacent have hurt both my business and me.

. . . I've learned the hard way that the times that I have been complacent have hurt both my business and me . . .

• Keeping Your Tools Sharp

I continually educate my team and myself. My father taught me the importance of education at a young age. I have done it for so long now that it is a part of who I am. I want to learn as much as possible and thrive on staying as sharp as I can.

. . . I want to learn as much as possible and thrive on staying as sharp as I can . . .

• What Is A Good Tenant?

A good tenant is the one that you don't hear about. They live in the house that never seems to be a problem and always pay their rent on time. I have quite a few of these and I try to show my appreciation to them.

• Call Them Residents, Not Tenants

I have instituted a policy in my organization that says simply, "we have residents, not tenants". This simple change in a word brings with it a level of respect that is felt by both the resident and my management team.

. . . "we have residents, not tenants" . . .

• What Kind Of Landlord Do I Want?

I treat people the way I want to be treated. I ask myself, how would I want my landlord to act?

• What Property Management Is Necessary?

Property management is a necessary element in this business. Even if you don't want to manage your properties yourself, you must understand and appreciate all of the functions that are involved.

. . . Even if you don't want to manage your properties yourself, you must understand and appreciate all of is the functions that are involved . . .

• Managing Residents

Managing residents is a unique talent. I have been fortunate to learn from a member of my team whom I believe to be among the best in the field. My ability to work with her to establish the policies we abide by has been very beneficial. These policies along with tips and things to avoid will be in one of my later publications.

• **Maintaining Property**

Maintaining my properties is crucial to my success. The ability to set my rental properties up in the beginning for easy long-term maintenance is one reason I have enjoyed the success that I have. I am producing a publication on property maintenance in the near future.

. . . The ability to set my rental properties up in the beginning for easy long-term maintenance is one reason I have enjoyed the success that I have . . .

The SLUMLORD

In stark contrast to what I'm offering here, I paint the picture below of a hypothetical villain – also known as a slumlord just to illustrate the kind of image that some possess in the rental business that I'm doing my best to distance myself from.

Where did we go wrong?

How in the world did rental property owners get such a horrible reputation? Did some landlord along the way really do that much damage? Do all property owners deserve to suffer due to the unscrupulous actions of a few? Stay with me here, I am just getting warmed up. Do the real slumlords have any idea of the additional rules, regulations and just plain baloney the rest of us have to put up with due to their business practices? Are they even remotely aware of the pain and suffering they cause their residents? Do they care? I doubt it.

Somewhere along the way things got way off base to the point now where many or all property owners are assumed guilty until proven innocent. What the hell happened?

When I look back at my early years in this business, I can say with all honesty that I had no idea how things would turn out. I had no way of seeing the great future that property ownership would bring. What I had was two things going for me: 1) I had great faith in my Dad and his vision for what our company could become and; 2) I knew that I would not be a slumlord. Being a new homebuilder and land developer by trade, I had only heard of the slumlord stories at the cocktail parties. When we started acquiring older homes I was even a little embarrassed to tell my other builder buddies what I was doing. Their jokes of me being a slumlord were ongoing and relentless as only your best buddies can dish out. Somehow all of their ribbing was feeding my deep desire to be different. I knew that building our rental portfolio was the right move for us, and I knew that I could find a way to do it right, so my pursuit began with a clear understanding of what I didn't want to become: a slumlord.

Slumlords by definition don't care about anything else but lining their pockets with as much profits as possible. They are easily recognized for their actions are so easily recognized. I have a strong suspicion that every area has a few of them.

How do slumlords stay in business? Well, they typically will rent to people that the rest of us won't rent to. They don't bother with background and credit checks perhaps because of the rundown appearance of their properties, they know that they probably won't be getting anyone with good credit, so why bother? I suspect that even if they gather information about their renters, they probably don't call any references because they already know that what's been put down is probably fraudulent, anyway. The most obvious tip off about them is that these are the same owners that will not make necessary repairs to their own properties. When things do go wrong with the property, you can count on them to take the cheapest and easiest way out no matter what the repair may be. Covering up problems seems to be the norm for them. Somehow they have bought into the theory of just keeping their properties rented for as much rent as possible until it falls down around them. Some slumlords show up in person to collect the rent for the purpose of counting heads in their apartments. They knock on the door, enter the unit and start counting how many occupants are there. They base that months rent on how many people they see and collect it right then. Wow, you talk about a crappy business model. Their residents are not residents at all. I would suspect they aren't much of anything to the slumlord. They aren't really people. They are just sources of temporary revenue. They don't stay long and always leave frustrated and angry. The municipalities know all the slumlords by name and which properties they own, as they are the ones that all the complaints come in about. They are probably in court so much, they could justify purchasing a monthly parking pass! Somehow these slumlords keep getting people to rent from them and avoid being run out of town.

I can tell you with 100% certainty I am not a slumlord. I will also hazard a guess that due to the fact you are reading this book you are not interested in being a slumlord either.

Let's review how slumlord behavior compares with what I do as a bona fide, upstanding landlord so you are clear about the differences:

- **Slumlords rent to anyone**

As a comparison, I rent to people that are qualified to comfortably make rent payments and will treat my property with respect. I check and verify all background, references, and other information for security risks before going ahead with any rental agreement. When an applicant passes my due diligence requirements, I ask that every resident follow established behavior guidelines. Putting someone in a house just to have it occupied is not an option for me.

- **Slumlords do not make repairs**

I make repairs to my properties as needed. This is required for so many reasons. First and foremost is the safety and security of my residents. Next to that there is quiet enjoyment and general satisfaction. If their repairs and concerns are dealt with efficiently they will stay longer, be more apt to pay their rent on time and generally be easier to deal with. Then there is protecting my investment. There are a lot of times when protecting my investment has cost me more then just fixing the immediate problem. For example I find the toilet has been leaking. I do more than just fix the leaky toilet. I will poke and prod to see what damage that leaking toilet has caused, then repair everything that needs to be repaired. I have to say that only a true slumlord does not care about their property. I will not have a property putting me at risk. Now I do have a couple of properties that I am not making major improvements to because I think at some point in time it will be cost effective to tear them down and build something new. These properties continue to be maintained for the safety of the resident at all times and the rent reflects the condition they are in.

- **Slumlords may collect cash in person**

I don't collect rent in person at the residence nor do I make it a practice to count occupants. I expect the residents that I do business with to be adults and treat them as such. I have had situations where this did not bode well for me in the end but refuse to let a few bad residences lower my standards.

- **Slumlords have no respect for the resident**

I hold a belief that my residents are my customers, period. Residents are the most important part of my business because without them, my business would not exist. I will show my residents the respect a valued customer deserves and do my best to assure they are as comfortable in their home as they can be. This approach has proven to bring with it many benefits, the least of which is that I sleep well at night knowing people are being treated right.

- **Slumlords are at war with the authorities**

I deal with several different cities and counties on a regular basis. Within each of these municipalities are numerous inspectors, code violation people and the like. I can tell you that at times I feel unfairly picked on. On occasion, I feel that my properties get singled out to make the government's numbers look good. They know that when they send a complaint to my office, it will get taken care of. For example, if a letter to clean up the alley behind a property within 5 days is sent to my office, I'll take a truck and dump trailer along with a crewmember with me to get it cleaned up. When I arrive at the location, I am frequently surprised that not only is my property not the worst offender, but actually about average for the area itself. So why would they send me the notice and not my neighbors? My theory is that they know it will be taken care of if they ask me and that helps their own numbers. This is just my belief but one that seems to happen a lot. I will also continue to take care of anything I am asked to do; within reason of course as I believe it is in my best interest to not have the municipality against me.

I WILL NOT BE A SLUMLORD!

Summing Up

Holding property for a significant time as a business proposition will enable investment tax and appreciation opportunities to fully mature. In doing so, the astute real estate investor will be granted other long term benefits that will make his investment one of the most flexible and profitable of all investment vehicles.

To hold property a long time -- long enough to maximize all available benefits demands becoming a skillful landlord who has the right mindset, time available, and a whole host of skills including: financial, observational, learning, people, resourcefulness, flexibility, patience, fortitude, do-whatever-it-takes, on-going management, and management team building savvy to succeed.

CHAPTER 6

Buying, Selling And Holding At The Right Time, For The Right Reasons

I purchased this place in the year 2000 for $63,000 and thought that I had hit a homerun. This was a simple 3-bedroom, one-and half-bath house with three garages and an unfinished basement right in the sweet spot of my target market neighborhood. The house needed a little more than the cosmetic fixing. There was no major way to increase value within the house itself, for example by adding bedrooms other than my normal updating of the kitchen, baths, flooring and paint. The initial repair and remodeling cost approximately $30,000 – an amount that put me at the limit of what I wanted to invest and still have positive rental cash flow.

I thought this property would for sure be a home run because of the three garages that needed no renovation and that came with the house - a two car attached garage in the front of the house and a small two car detached garage behind it. I thought these garages would be very attractive to good quality renters and because of this, would virtually guarantee no vacancies for as long as we owned the house far into the future. In fact, I may even have thought the three garages might enable us to easily raise the rent over time due to high demand. How can you say I was wr wr wr, wr wr wr WRONG?

Unfortunately, I'd have to say that this investment turned out to be the homerun that got away. I should either have never purchased the house or should have torn down the extra garage space from the beginning. All that garage space that I was so confident would be a bonus turned out to be an incredible pain that did not raise our average rent. The residents that were attracted to this property all came with the same challenges – they all had an excessive amount of junk! The excess garage space attracted junk cars and garbage like flies to honey. In addition, the late night pounding and banging on our renter's projects that the garages made possible upset all the neighbors that in turn kept complaints streaming into my office non-stop. This same scenario played out over and over again, year after year. We tried everything we could think of short of demolishing the extra space. We even rented the place to one of my employees for a period of time and we used the garages for our own storage, but this didn't work out well either. The only resolution seemed to be to sell. I looked at selling it a couple of times over the years but finally did in 2008 for $195,000 – more than doubling what we initially paid for it over a span of 8 years. We got lucky and made a nice sales profit in addition to the rental income and depreciable tax benefits, but it was a very frustrating experience that I still can't seem to shake off.

In This Chapter

Knowing when to buy, sell, and hold are functions of the real estate investment model you follow; specifically, the types of houses you make investments in, the types of investment benefits you seek and extent of your personal involvement in the practice. Here I discuss how I apply my real estate investment model in guiding these buy, sell and hold decisions.

When Is It The Right Time To Buy?

I have learned that any time you find an investment house that fits your criteria, it is right the time to buy. Opportunities usually don't come along on schedule. They come along when they come along on somebody else's schedule. This is the reason it is so important to have thought out ahead of time what your criteria is so you can more easily recognize what are the best opportunities for you.

. . . Opportunities usually don't come along on schedule . . .

I know what works in my market. I know how long certain projects will take my crews to complete and how much work I have lined up ahead of them. When I am looking for a project, I know what it is that I'm looking for and when I would want to start it. In some cases, I have been able to time the acquisition to coincide with when I can get to the work.

Many projects have come to me when I wasn't necessarily looking for them. If my crews were too busy at the time, I either made sure it was a good enough deal that it could wait or passed on it all together. Always remember the holding costs you are incurring while a house sits with nothing getting done to it. The problem with all of this hypothetical timing advice is that it is difficult to implement. The reality is that when I was going great guns with three busy crews and subcontractors, the buying seemed to be in spurts. One month my father would buy three houses at foreclosure sales, then we would pick up another one from a bank or a realtor; then the next month, we wouldn't purchase a thing. The acquisition systems that were in place did not stop, but the results would vary. As you can see, the timing and scheduling is challenging when your purchasing opportunities are unpredictable.

. . . Always remember the holding costs you are incurring while a house sits with nothing getting done to it . . .

WARNING!

You cannot lower your standards just to keep your rehabilitation machine going. I have made mistakes several times over by doing this. I have purchased a few houses in the buzz of activity because I didn't want our momentum to stop -- houses that did not fit right into my criteria but were close. In hindsight, I may have been better off adjusting my rehabilitation crews and passing on the so-so deals.

. . . In hindsight, I may have been better off adjusting my rehabilitation crews and passing on the so-so deals . . .

When Is It Time To Sell?

When done correctly, you can sell any time and make money. This is the beauty of following my system. I have made money on the buy (on paper) and on the initial increase in value (on paper), giving me the option to sell anytime I want. I am not waiting for tax benefits or appreciation to make it possible for me to sell and get out, nor do I have to hope for some big upswing in the market. Market conditions will certainly give me an indication of when the optimum time to sell may be, and certainly when it would be the easiest. Even in tougher economic climates, though I have sold houses on contracts, lease options and even taken other items of value in on trade.

. . . you can sell any time and make money. This is the beauty of following my system . .

What And How Long To Hold?

After spending time searching for, purchasing, planning and renovating the houses we acquire and fix up, holding – which is to say managing and maintaining property is what our company mainly does. We usually hold for a long time until the time is right to sell. As I've described again and again in this book, we're in this investment business for the long haul, so we can maximize all the benefits we can, and optimize the timing of our buying and selling.

. . . We usually hold for a long time until the time is right to sell . . .

During our holding period -- frequently many years, market conditions change. Specifically as to our houses and the neighborhoods in which our houses are found, our client's families mature, their job situations change, relationships change, real estate values and rental prices change, and our property neighborhoods improve and decline.

We've learned as a company to re-evaluate each of our properties on an on-going basis to determine which houses to keep and which to sell relative to our holding period base of properties. A few years back I instituted an ongoing grading system on all of our existing properties. I involved 5 of the key people in our organization (finance, operations, management, maintenance, customer service) so that we had a good all around point of view. Using a scale of A, B, C or D, we graded each property. D's were houses that we would sell off judging that they had proven to be more trouble than they were worth. A's were properties that we would keep. The idea was to periodically conduct this evaluation (at least once a year) so that we always kept the highest quality properties for ourselves as well as making room for our stock to always be kept fresh and at the highest standards with the fewest problems. We did this every year because conditions change over time.

. . . Using a scale of A, B, C or D, we graded each property. D's were houses that we would sell. A's were properties that we would keep . . .

The way this worked as a practical matter was when a house that was graded as a D became vacant, I looked to see what current market conditions were, met with my accountant and generally opened up the discussion with our key managers as to whether or not it was a good time for us to sell the property. If the answer was yes, we looked for the best method to do this with the best possible candidate.

The point is that as long as we are positioned in the properties well, we have the flexibility to do whatever we want, whenever we want – a stance that works very well with real estate cycles. The question as to how long to hold, therefore is a complex one that can only be answered relative to market conditions, our business model, and our long term goals.

. . . as long as we are positioned in the properties well, we have the flexibility to do whatever we want, whenever we want – a stance that works very well with real estate cycles . . .

Summing Up

I buy investment property whenever I see something that fits my real estate investment model no matter what real estate cycle we find ourselves in; I sell whenever it is most advantageous for me to do so by many optional measures of personal advantage; and I make a very efficient business out of mastering the holding of property to optimize both the buying and selling of property.

. . . I make a very efficient business out of mastering the holding of property to optimize both the buying and selling of property. . .

I'm always positioned to buy, sell, and hold property, whatever is called for in line with following my business model. Almost from the first moment I buy property, I'm positioned to sell it. As time passes, my selling position gets significantly more favorable. The fact that I can sell my investment property whenever I decide to do so, however, doesn't mean I will do so. In fact, I have a great reluctance to sell any property I acquire . . . unless I am forced to do so by circumstances. I will usually only sell if neighborhood conditions deteriorate, my residents desire to purchase, or my personal circumstances require raising funds. Other than that, I focus most of my time on either searching for new properties to purchase, or perfecting my skills at holding investment property as a landlord.

CHAPTER 7

Choices I've Made As A Professional Home Investor: What I Do And What I Don't Do

I purchased this house for the sole purpose of reselling it quickly – a speculative practice people now call a flip. The house was located in a very nice community a little beyond the boundaries of my rental market. It was the low cost, minimal restoration classic cosmetic fixer opportunity –that is now so well publicized. All that this house really needed was the yard cleaned up and a fresh new coat of paint on the outside; and a few minor repairs, new kitchen counter tops and new paint on the interior. All of this cleanup and cosmetic touchup took just a few weeks to complete. With the total cost of the house and all rehabilitation being $165,000 our selling price of $225,000, it worked out well; but this is not why it was such a good flip.

This house was the perfect flip due to the backup options it presented. What I mean by this is if it didn't work out as a flip – for example if we couldn't sell it within a short time, we were ready, willing and able to place it in our rental inventory because it fulfilled nearly all of the criteria we normally use to select homes for rentals.

How close were we to having this not work out as a flip? We were very close. When I put the house on the market for sale, I gave it a 3-month marketing time with one of the best realtors I knew. In those first three months, he had a couple of interested parties and it seemed that a sale was going to work out soon, so we extended the marketing time another couple of months. As we came to the end of this five-month period, I was just ready to pull the plug on the marketing and make it available to my property manager to rent when a solid offer was presented, which we ultimately accepted. Would we have been okay if we had just rented it instead of flipping? Yes. The point of the story is if I'm going to buy a house with the idea of flipping it, I make sure the numbers work out so the house is able to carry itself as a rental in the event it doesn't sell. This is the way I've decided to do business. You may decide that this makes sense for you too.

In This Chapter

I concentrate all my wisdom and learning here about my successful real estate investment model in the form of boiled-down-to-the essence, bottom-line, core-beliefs, and black-and-white absolute advice. Yes there is some overlap and repetition here with the ideas presented in previous chapters.

The Overall Business Model Of Lowering Risk And Maximizing Options

I buy houses that I can make money on in 3 different ways. I work very hard to purchase houses that fit all three business models, but I am not always successful in that. I will break down the three money-making options and you will see the importance of having all of them as options.

• Fix & Flip Now

Oh, the famous fix & flip model that worked so well before all the hype and TV shows. I am sure that I was not the only professional real estate investor in the country that cringed every time one of these shows came on the air. Back in the good old days, people were fascinated to find out that I would buy their house in as-is condition, giving them an option they didn't think they had. Then came all the hype. Fast forward a few years and sellers thought they had gold mines and the prices went through the roof. Every one and their brother thought they could make a fortune purchasing a fixer property and throwing a coat of paint on it. This is what the TV shows were telling them. This combination of events screwed up a pretty sweet deal I had. When I was one of the few people around that bought fixer properties, I had a lot more opportunities available.

• Fix & Rent Out Indefinitely (A properties only)
Purchasing, repairing and renting "ugly duckling" houses is the basic model I have always followed. For most of these houses I had no plans to sell when I purchased them and have no plans to sell now. I actually work very hard to protect them as a valuable asset. After all, building a long-term viable investment is my goal.

As a company we have graded each property with our own A, B, C & D system.

A's are the true keepers. B's are keepers but still need a few things done. C's are ok for now but for any number of reasons is not a desirable keeper. D's are the dogs -- the ones that we want to sell as soon as the opportunity presents itself. This is a little tough on some of them as the market, area or existing financing dictates when we can get rid of some of these houses. This grading system keeps us very aware of which properties are on the chopping block so to speak.

The A's and B's make up the majority of our houses most of the time. These are the ones that we will continue to provide as homes for our residents. They just keep going. As for the C's and D's, they are always up for review. When one becomes vacant, a discussion is initiated as to what we could do to elevate it higher on the scale and we look at the current market conditions for a possible sale. At this time, when we have more or less reached our inventory limit, I only look at new purchases that have "A" potential. Upgrading to as many "A" units as possible fulfills my goal of always upgrading my current inventory of houses so that I can keep them filled with happy residents.

• Sell Only When the Right Opportunity Presents Itself

Our goal is to own our homes as long-term investments for as long as it's beneficial to do so. We will only sell our homes if they are no longer financially beneficial to us, or if our residents would benefit by becoming owners of the homes they have rented from us over a significant period of time. A house I purchase some 10 plus years ago is a prime example of this. It is right next to an old gas station just off one of the main roads in town. I remodeled it right after acquiring it and then once again in later years. The old gas station next door was remodeled into a lube and oil service and added a coffee stand. These are quite popular in my area. The couple that runs the service station rented the house a couple of years ago and really enjoyed being right next door to their place of business. The next thing I knew, they were making an offer to purchase the house. This was not a house that we were planning on selling anytime soon, but it seemed to be the best time to do it. Who better to own the house than the same peoples involved in the business next door? The end result has been that the house looks great. The people have really taken pride in the house and have turned it into a beautiful home. This was the right time for the new owners and definitely the best thing for the community. It was just time for the house to have a homeowner in it and it worked out well for us too.

• Fix, Rent Out Now, & Flip Later

This is the mother lode – the crème de la crème of real estate investing! When I found this model and developed the systems to support it, the stars in the heavens began to line up.

. . . When I found this model and developed the systems to support it, the stars in the heavens began to line up . . .

Find the "ugly duckling" that you can renovate in a way to substantially increase its value both as a rental and when sold. Rent it to good, deserving residents for a period of time (this has been as short as several months to as many as 15 years) and then sell. The sale of these well maintained, updated homes bring top dollar to proud homeowners. I am telling you that it doesn't get any better than this!

Buying The Right Kind Of Neighborhood - Basic, Not Romantic

My neighborhoods are not romantic and not scary – they are "just right". This may make you think of Goldie Locks and The Three Bears children story – where the fluffy, way too soft bed is like the fancy, romantic neighborhood – it's pretty to look at and nice to live in yourself, but no place to make any money with rental properties. For the kinds of homes you find in these kinds of neighborhoods, it's just too hard to make the numbers work out so that you have a positive cash flow (covering all ongoing carrying costs of the house), without initially putting an enormous amount of money into the house.

The way too hard bed is referring to those scary neighborhoods that every area has -- the ones that you do not want to be in too long in the daylight, let alone at night. I can tell you from experience that it is just like the bed choice -- way too hard to make any money in these areas for me -- hard to find good residents and equally difficult to sell when the time comes.

When Goldie Locks found the bed that was just right, she sighed, relaxed and went right to sleep. In similar manner, when you find those neighborhoods that make sense financially and you are comfortable working in, your life will be a lot easier. Now this is not to say that these areas don't have their share of challenges at times, but they don't stay there forever.

. . . when you find those neighborhoods that make sense financially and you are comfortable working in, your life will be a lot easier . . .

My description of the optimum neighborhood may seem a little rough, but here goes. These areas are where the "lunch pail" workers live -- basic, hard working folks of all ages living a modest, middle class lifestyle. In this day and age, a lot of these folks are single parents as well. One of the keys to why these neighborhoods work so well is the easy availability of their jobs. Lunch pail jobs don't pay as well but are easy to find, easy to get hired for, easy to leave to find another, and therefore typically have less risk associated. This gives some stability to the neighborhood.

. . . the optimum neighborhood . . are where the "lunch pail" workers live – basic, hard working folks of all ages living a modest, middle class lifestyle . . .

Buying At The Optimal Time

The secret about buying houses at an optimal time is . . . there is no optimal time. It's always good. I can find houses to suit my criteria in any market condition. Think about it. There are always people that need to sell their homes. Circumstances beyond their control such as job transfers and illnesses force them to sell when they may not have been planning on it. Even if it may not be an optimal time in the general real estate market to sell, it certainly is an optimal time to sell for those sellers who need it sold immediately. The U.S. housing market is large and diverse enough to contain people of all social and economic classes who have a consistent and persistent range of housing supply and demand needs most all of the time. Such a market is now and almost always ready to provide for the entrepreneur who is ready to amass a fortune in rental real estate. Having clear guidelines and goals about what it is that you want as an investor is the key to going out and purchasing good rentals. Combine those guidelines with the knowledge and experience/scars I will share with you and buying is right anytime.

. . . there is no optimal time. It's always good . . .

Buying The Ugliest Lady Or Gentleman On The Block

I love the "Ugly Duckling" house. This is where I make my money. How many guys do you know that get excited when they drive by a boarded-up house? I mean whenever I see something like this, the chances are good that I will probably come to a screeching halt, crane my neck all around looking for the house address, run back to the office to look up any information I can find about it, and start the process of finding the owner. Heck, I even know the City of Tacoma's color codes for the writing on the plywood boarded up material, so I know why the house was boarded up in the first place. But hey, boarded up places are not the only ugly ducklings out there. Really, they are everywhere. Once you start looking for them, they will jump right out at you. It is just like when you buy the brand new car in the model and color you've never seen before; the next day you'll notice six of them on your way to work.

. . . How many guys do you know that get excited when they drive by a boarded-up house? . . .

Renovating To Suit Market Needs, Limited By Property Management Criteria

I make the improvements needed to attract and keep good residents. Renovating rental properties requires a different skill and mindset than remodeling your own house. I often refer to it as putting on a different set of glasses. First I have to look at the house for exactly what it is -- an investment. Then I renovate only those areas that will increase rental and overall value. These steps will probably be very different than if you were personally going to live in the house yourself, and they are the only ones you should concern yourself with. There are few, if any exceptions to this rule. Once you are personally involved emotionally, you are not making business decisions.

. . . Renovating rental properties requires . . . putting on a different set of glasses . . .

Smart Renovations

Smart renovations such as modernizing kitchens, baths and floor plan, adding bedrooms and garages are the ones that will increase value. Smart is often different than cute or nice. Now at times they can be the same and I work hard to make all my renovations look as good as possible but remember what set of glasses I have on here. I make only the renovations that will add value now and later -- including things that will make my maintenance easier over time. Modernizing kitchens and baths will get my houses rented faster and keep the residents happier, but bedrooms add immediate dollars to my account. In my rental market each bedroom I add increases rental income by an average of ±$100 per month. So when I purchase a 2-bedroom house and add 2 more bedrooms in the attic space you can see that over time it makes one heck of a difference.

. . . Modernizing kitchens and baths will get my houses rented faster and keep the residents happier, but bedrooms add immediate dollars to my account . . .

The Positive Cash Flow Limitations

The rent amount has to cover the house payment. This is so important in order to build a business. The rent amount you are expecting has got to be at least equal to the amount of your underlying mortgage. Unexpected challenges will come up from time to time and eat up your cash reserves, so you can't be using them to make up the payment difference every month. This step is key in building a business rather than just a house of cards. It's the difference between my business and 100 other so-called real estate investors that have come and gone in my market over the years.

. . . The rent amount you are expecting has got to be at least equal to the amount of your underlying mortgage . . .

Renting For The Optimal Time

I continually evaluate my properties to see which ones may need to be sold. When my business got to a certain size I instituted a grading policy on the rental houses. There were 5 of us that each graded the individual houses from A – D from our own perspective. The grades were then combined and discussed before they were assigned. Grade values were:

A - is a keeper with no plans to sell
B – is a keeper with reservations
C - could be a keeper with modifications
D – is a DOG! SELL when the opportunity arises

Now this grading curve can and has changed from time to time as the areas and the market changes. What it has done for my business, however is to give us a plan to base our decisions upon when houses become vacant.

. . . Grade values . . . give us a plan to base our decisions upon when houses become vacant . . .

Selling At The Optimal Time

I keep a close eye on my market conditions at all times to determine what, if anything can be done, and when it may be optimal to sell. Watching the market combined with the following the grading system I just showed you takes a lot of the guess work out of these decisions. I run my business like a business.

. . . I run my business like a business . . .

Property Management The Right Way

I have a great team and proper systems in place to manage and maintain all of our properties. Good property management comes down to putting in place and following a series of systems to get everything done the way you want them to be done, when they need to be done. Whether you learn this from me or someone else doesn't matter as much as the fact that you do need to learn them. Novice investors get themselves into a whole heap of trouble trying to do this on their own. You must know the landlord/tenant laws in your area and be prepared to uphold them. I have been very fortunate in that over 15 years ago my current Chief Operating Officer joined my business and brought with her years of property management experience.

. . . Good property management comes down to putting in place and following a series of systems to get everything done the way you want them to be done, when they need to be done . . .

Even with all of this knowledge, we still had to learn about systematizing our business to run more smoothly. After years of several of us running around like chickens with our heads cut off and doing nothing but putting out fires all day, I finally wised up and developed the proper systems that were needed. To learn about systems, three of us went through the E-Myths extensive coaching program over a period of several years and this has been instrumental in our business. This coaching is based on Michael Gerbers E-Myth book series. I suggest you read them. In addition to establishing and developing the systems to smoothly run my business, this training has given me the freedom to do to other things such as writing this book!

Mistakes, More Mistakes, And Even More Mistakes – Don't Do What I Did

Here is the easiest, cheapest education you will ever get in simple terms. Learn from my mistakes so you don't have to make them yourself. If you choose to do some of the things I talk about here then you will at least be making those decisions based on more information.

. . . Don't Do What I Did . . .

• Don't Be Upside Down

I have houses rented out with negative cash flow that I can't sell for what I have put into them. Negative cash flow sucks. There is no nice way to say that. Houses that I purchased with only one logical way out, which was to sell, put me in a bad position when the market took a turn downwards. Right now I am not alone in this. The current market conditions have a lot of the "fix & flip" people really wishing they had just kept watching the others doing it on TV. If you are in this predicament, then I wish you all the best. Hopefully you are not buried so far that you can hold on until the market heats up again. I have had a few that I have had to sell at a loss -- I mean a real loss where it was worth it to get out to stop the bleeding. These are no fun and it takes a few good deals to make up for them. All of them are learning lessons though. Seems I learn a lot the hard way.

. . .Negative cash flow sucks. There is no nice way to say that . . .

• Don't Be Perfect

I have had stretches of good luck that made me lazy and complacent with my systems. Lets face it. We are all human and when things are going good, I for one tend to get lazy. I share this with you because running a business requires that you stay focused and on task. Just because there are no evictions or problem residences right now does not mean that you are immune from the challenges forever. If you are in this business for as long a period of time as I have been, probably you will have most of the experiences that I am sharing with you. Your area is not that different than mine. Your residents are not better or more qualified. You may have just been lucky so far. This is a good thing, but stay prepared and ahead of the curve. You will thank me later.

- **Don't Wind Up Being A No Equity Landlord**

I have houses with no equity that I have no choice but to keep renting. These few houses have all been a part of that painful learning curve that I am trying to save you from. They seemed like good deals at the time, but when all was said and done, I wished I had never got involved at all. I have been surprised by too much work needed. I've also been caught with too many projects going on at once where one or two had to sit and wait to get work done. Sometimes, time can be the worst enemy of all in this business as it can quickly erode away the equity you once had. So in the end, I have houses that only make sense to keep renting, taking away the flexibility that I strive for.

. . . Sometimes, time can be the worst enemy of all in this business as it can quickly erode away the equity you once had . . .

- **Don't Over-finance Later**

I really wish that I could tell you that I have always followed all of my own advice and never pulled more money out of a house than what the rent could carry, but I cannot. In the heat of the moment when my other building and land development projects were going well, I did refinance a little too much on a few properties. That is not to say that they went backwards a whole lot, but they certainly are not in as profitable a situation as they once were. I can't even say whether or not I would do the same thing again, but I can tell you that I am a lot more careful now. I think long and hard before messing with a good positive cash flow.

. . . I think long and hard before messing with a good positive cash flow . . .

- **Don't Pay Too Much For The House**

I have paid too much for houses when I initially under-estimated how much was wrong with them – the furnace that needed replacing or the electrical system that was in worse shape than I expected. This is depressing because these surprises have come at the worst times. Fortunately, they have happened less frequently with more business experience.

• Don't Improve The Wrong Things

I have spent time and money making improvements that in the end did not add enough value to make it worthwhile. In retrospect, I had to learn how my residents would live in my rental houses before I knew what improvements made the most sense. Take the dining room for instance. Soon after going back inside, several of my rental houses after they were occupied, it occurred to me that the residents in my market did not use the dining room as it was originally intended. More often than not, it was being utilized as an office, kids play room or even another bedroom. This being the case, it was obvious that spending money on dining room chandeliers was a complete waste of resources. This is just one example of making sure the money spent on improving the property is of value to the residence.

. . . In retrospect, I had to learn how my residents would live in my rental houses before I knew what improvements made the most sense . . .

• Don't Buy The Wrong House

I have purchased houses that I shouldn't have usually at times when I felt I had to keep the momentum going to keep several crews working. Had I been able to stick more to my game plan, things would be easier now. I ventured into neighborhoods that I wish I hadn't and bought a couple of houses that needed more extensive work than I would have liked. Take it from me. Stay on your plan if you have one; and if you don't have one, make one. Buy only the houses that make economic sense and you have good feelings about. If it doesn't feel right in the beginning, odds are it will only get worse.

. . . If it doesn't feel right in the beginning, odds are it will only get worse . . .

• Don't Tear Down And Rebuild

Tearing down and rebuilding single-family houses (one for one) in my market is cost prohibitive. Purchasing a house with the plan of tearing it down and building another in its place does work in some markets, but not mine yet. There are still enough building lots available and the cost of getting rid of the old house is very expensive. The dump fees have climbed enormously over the last few years. In addition to that, you must go through all of the asbestos and lead abatement processes before you can tear the house down. This adds a lot of costs to the building site you end up with. If the zoning changes so that you can rebuild more units, it may be a different situation entirely. I purchased an old house a couple of years ago in an area that was recently rezoned to encourage multifamily units. I tore down the house and built a 7-unit townhouse building on the site. In this case, it was worth the exercise of tearing down the house to go from one house to seven units.

• Don't Add Another Story

I will not add another story on to an existing house in my market again. Mere words cannot express how painfully true this statement is. I made a huge mistake awhile back that I am still paying for. I purchased a house that needed rehabilitation and at the time it seemed like a good idea to add another story to it. This would give the house an additional two bedrooms, one of them being a nice master bedroom with a bath.

The plan was fine -- there was nothing wrong with the plan. It was the implementation of that plan along with the costs associated with it that caused me all the problems. I spent way too much money. I had the wrong contractor on the job. The job took way too long. I did not pay close enough attention to the project in the beginning. I could go on, but my stomach is starting to hurt. The end result was that I have a house that is over built for the neighborhood and I can't sell for what I have into it. It is currently rented out and has a negative cash flow. Some day I will be able to get rid of the house, but I will never get rid of the bad taste in my mouth.

. . . I made a huge mistake awhile back . . . I spent way too much money . . .

• Don't Doll Up And Gingerbread Your Rental Houses Like You Would Your Own House

Please do not misunderstand me. I hold my residents in the highest regard and in no way think that I am better than them. I know that without them I cannot do what I do. I also do the best that I can to provide them with clean, safe and efficient housing. On the other hand, I also know that my lifestyle differs from theirs in some major ways and a lot of these differences are the differences between owning and renting. Although I strive to have my residents take pride of ownership in their rental home, it is still not the same as being the one that pays the mortgage. The difference between being an owner and a renter is one that I have learned to respect. It helps remind me of the all-important fact that this is a business and must be run that way.

. . . I . . .do the best that I can to provide . . . clean, safe and efficient housing . . .

• Don't Get Emotionally Attached To The Houses Or The Residents

I cannot afford to have emotional ties to my investments. They are like chess pieces on a board. Business is business and emotions have to be controlled. Sure I have houses that I like better than others, but that plays a minor role in my decisions. I am not emotionally attached to any of them. There are actually quite a few houses that I would just a soon not own, but they make very good sense to own from a business standpoint. So as you can see, emotions can sway you in both directions. Just keep them under control and always look at the numbers. I have been accused of emotional involvement due to the fact that I trust my instincts. I can't agree with these accusations because I differentiate between the two. I don't trust my emotions, but I do trust my instincts. My instincts are learned, valuable skills that are based on my experiences. When I have gone against them in the past, it has usually hurt my bank account.

Want to know what I mean by emotional involvement about houses? Let me tell you a story about how I got emotionally involved in buying the home I now live in. This is what you don't want to do when buying rental property. The home I share with my bride and our 5 teenage children is not in the same neighborhood as my rental houses. It is close by and in the same city, but in a totally different part of town. Now when I purchased our current waterfront home a couple of years ago, I was definitely "emotionally involved". I fell in love with both the house and its location. I pinch myself everyday and give thanks for the opportunity to live in a place so beautiful – this is something that I am not used to when it comes to houses. I don't feel the same about any of my rental houses. I hope you are noticing a significant difference in my outlook between my personal home and my investment houses. This is so important to understand and it is one of the biggest mistakes I see investors making. Please do not misunderstand my intentions here. I am not saying that my home is necessarily superior to my rental houses. This has nothing to do with it. The point is that I am emotionally connected with my personal home, as I'm sure you are. This is where my bride and I have our family and we both work very hard to have it as comfortable as possible. On the other hand, my investment houses need to first make sense financially and second be someone's home. I cannot allow my personal taste and emotions to dictate my investments. I am running a business and providing a service not personally living in every house. This "different set of glasses" needs to be in everything involved with the rental house. Exterior paint colors, decks and landscaping all have to be neutral and easily maintained. Interior paint is one color. Carpet, vinyl and counter tops are all in the neutral range with minimal patterns. The list can go on and on. The point is that everything is looked at differently than your own house. Have your "investor glasses" on when you are dealing with your rental houses. Keep the "rose colored" ones for home.

. . . I cannot allow my personal taste and emotions to dictate my investments . . .

- **Don't Micromanage – Be Careful Not To Overdo Things**

I have to let my teamwork within the systems that I have set up and I have to manage the systems. Developing the proper systems for my business to operate was one of the best things I ever did. I followed the E-myth philosophy that systems are both manageable and freeing. They have it figured out. All the hard work it takes to develop and continually innovate the systems is well worth it. With the appropriate systems in place, there is no need to micromanage. People will live up to what is expected of them and more. Before E-myth I was trying to manage the people working for me and it caused entirely too much stress on me and them. This is a lot better and I only wish I had been smart enough to do it earlier.

. . . Developing the proper systems for my business to operate was one of the best things I ever did . . .

- **Don't Rely Too Heavily On Banks**

Oh how I wish I had figured this one out sooner. When we started in our acquisition mode my father had excellent, well-established banking relationships. We used those to build our portfolio and all worked out well. It was not until the last few years that I started making more of an effort to seek out private investors and seller financing. I so wish I had done that earlier on. I can now see that relying so heavily on the banks was a mistake. The problem is that banks change the rules all the time and it throws my game plans out the window. Look at the state of banks today. They don't know whether they're coming or going. Add into that all the current government involvement that has made dealing with banks very risky. I have no doubt that I could build my portfolio again today or tomorrow, but if I had to start again from scratch, I'd rely far more heavily on investor and seller financing instead of banks.

. . . The problem is that banks change the rules all the time . . .

- **Don't Invest In Areas Or Things That You Can't Control – For Example Neighborhood Growth Based On Rumors**

I cannot let the newspapers and politics dictate where I invest. I am sure you don't have to think too hard to recognize what I'm referring to. These are the areas that are so popular during election time -- the neighborhoods that are being promised, again, to get all the police protection, and improvement funds to help them out. I learned this lesson from Tacoma's "Hilltop" neighborhood. Over fifteen years ago, real estate investors were telling me that this was the up and coming area. All the problems were going to be driven out (gangs, drug dealers and the like) and as a result, housing prices would sky rocket. Now I can attest to the fact that over the last fifteen years, this area has seen great improvement. What I can also attest to is that there were a lot of investors that lost along the way -- people who thought that salvation was just around the corner. Neighborhoods do not change that fast. I bought houses in that area then and in later years. Most of them I still own and rent out today. I am happy that I have them, but I am also glad that I did not over do it based on what the newspapers were saying years ago. I could have starved waiting for the big turn around.

- **Don't Buy And Hold Too Long**

I have to keep reminding myself that some of my houses have run their course and it may be time to sell. Once in awhile I will have a house that just seems to be ready to sell. I think it is more of a gut feeling than anything else, but it does happen. The house is just ready to be someone's permanent home -- ready for all of those special touches only a proud homeowner can give it. I know it sounds crazy, but it does happen.

- **Don't Make Improvements At The Wrong Time**

I'm constantly thinking about what makes sense to do and when. This is because improvements have the potential of helping or hurting the profitability of my business depending upon when they are done. I am always juggling market strength, lease termination times, maintenance crew cost, and time available for making improvements. All of my properties could have improvements and maintenance the next time they are vacant, but what determines my actions depends to some extent upon the strength of demand for my units and other market factors such as competition. Improvements have the potential of being adjusted a bit depending on the length of time my crew has between residents. All of the safety and important maintenance items are done right away while they are occupied, if possible. I have houses that have had a short list of "want to do's" for quite some time, but it's hard to justify doing these when I can have the house rented again right away without doing them. As you can see, the decisions of what to do and when are flexible. On the other hand, once I bite the bullet and decide to make improvements, the economic benefits may or may not manifest in a timely manner.

. . . what determines my actions depends to some extent upon the strength of demand for my units and other market factors . . .

- **Don't Allow Bad Precedents**

When something or someone is causing a problem, I have to take care of it right away or it will spread like a disease. This is especially true when problems take place in multi-family units. A bad or unhappy resident can influence the rest of the residents immediately because they live in such close proximity to one another. When there is a challenge in a multi-family unit, I insist that it be taken care of immediately. That same challenge in one of the many single-family houses gives me more time so that I can be a little more patient. The fact is that the majority of my residents are good, upstanding folks, but the few "problem residents" can consume most of my staff's time and energy.

- **Don't Defer Maintenance**

I have learned the hard way what items need immediate attention and what items can wait. Maintenance takes work, patience and some fairly unique skills. It can be a real pain to work on the house while there is a resident living there. I won't even go into how you get the job done while 2 toddlers and their dog are following you all around. Even though a lot of this maintenance is performed in less than ideal conditions, it is necessary in order to protect both the resident and my investment. Anything that has to do with the safety of the residents gets done immediately and to the best quality obtainable at the time. I say this because there are situations where I might fix the immediate problem and also note in the file that additional work needs to be done the next time the house is vacant. These notes are valuable to my planning in the future and are reviewed frequently.

. . . I have learned the hard way (that maintenance) is necessary to protect both the resident and my investment . . .

- **Don't Ignore The Signs Of Problem Residents**

I have buried my head in the sand and just hoped things would get better, but they never do until I deal with it. It seems I have had to continue to learn this lesson over and over again – that a problem does not get better on its own. A resident that is creating a challenge or is just unhappy for some reason, just doesn't go away even though I wish that they would. I usually have to dig in and figure out how to get things resolved.

. . . I have had to continue to learn this lesson over and over again – that a problem does not get better on its own . . .

- **Don't Avoid Doing Due Diligence When Selecting Contractors**

People have fooled me several times over the years that I should have never hired. Think about contractors in this way. There is a reason why most of them are not working for someone else. Take this statement as neither positive nor negative but just as a fact. The challenge is to figure out how you are going to best work with them or whether you can work with them at all. Do all the normal things that everyone else tells you to do before hiring a contractor. Check their license and bond, references, and do one more thing -- the one that I have found to be the most crucial of all. Have a conversation with them. Ask them questions about their last few jobs, their family and employees. This will tell you a lot about both their work and their work ethics. Things will not go exactly as planned on any remodel job, so it is vital that you have hired a contractor that you can work with through the challenges.

. . . Things will not go exactly as planned on any remodel job . . . so . . . figure out how you are going to best work with them or whether you can work with them at all . .

• **Don't Forget The Neighbors**
I have learned time and again to make an effort to get in the neighbor's good graces. Say hello and introduce yourself right away. Listen to the stories about the people who lived there before and assure them that although it is going to be a rental, you are invested in the neighborhood and care about it. This is what every neighbor wants to hear. Remember that these neighbors are your eyes and ears watching over your investment and can be an important asset.

. . . neighbors are your eyes and ears watching over your investment and can be an important asset . . .

• **Don't Buy A Swimming Pool**
I will not have a pool or pond in my area due to maintenance and liability. Pools are not as common in the Pacific Northwest as they are in other parts of the country and the Koi (colorful Japanese Carp) fish ponds were a fad that seems to have passed. In my market these are not assets because they make me worry more about the liability that comes along with them. Because of that, I avoid them. If pools and ponds are more common in your area, I would make darn sure your insurance carrier has good coverage.

• Don't Buy Too Many Garages

I had to finally sell a house that I had originally thought would be a great rental because of its 4-car garage. I was sorely disappointed to discover that it attracted nothing but trouble for me. This was a very interesting lesson for me to learn. I purchased a house in my target market that had both a 2-car attached garage and a 2-car detached garage. There was nothing special about the house itself – just a typical 3 bedroom, one and half bath; but I thought that all of the garage space would be of real value as a rental. Yikes, was I wrong. The residents that occupied it over the years always started out fine, but things would go downhill every time. The broken down cars and junk were attracted to these garages like some kind of magnetic force. I went through this experience several times over and all with the same results. This repeated experience no matter who was involved would, in turn make my investment look terrible and disturb the neighbors, generating complaints to my office. So the conclusion that I arrived at after several years was to sell this house to a proud homeowner and chalk it up to experience. Too much garage space, I learned, can actually be a detriment.

. . . broken down cars and junk were attracted to these garages like some kind of magnetic force . . .

• Don't Buy Old Houses That Have Been Converted To Multi-Family Units

I will not buy multi-family units that were not originally built that way. I like houses that look and feel normal. Now I realize that the term "normal" is relative to my market. Maybe I should say that I don't like "odd" setups in houses or multi-family units. Some of the older homes in my area were converted into multi-family units many years ago, apparently without a whole lot of thought given to their functionality. The long sidewalk that leads to the door that gets you to the cramped stairwell is so small there is no way to get a couch or a queen size bed up to the upper unit, not to mention the half a kitchen and shower that could only be used if the resident is under 4'10" tall. Can you understand why these are features, "situations" and properties that don't interest me?

. . . I don't like "odd" setups in houses or multi-family units . . .

• Don't Buy Over Improved Property – You'll Just Have To Make Costly "Adjustments"

Residents that live in my investment houses do not have the same priorities as I do when it comes to the house. A high standard of maintenance has a lot less value to them. Landscaping is a prime example of this. Fancy plants that need watering and care have no place in my rental houses yard because the average resident will not take care of these and the yard will end up looking like a mess.

. . . Fancy plants (and other high maintenance items) . . . have no place in my rental houses . . . because the average resident will not take care of these . . .

Knowing this, I get rid of these types of features right after purchasing. My goal is to make it as easy as possible for the resident to maintain the house and still fit well in the neighborhood. Large wood decks and planter boxes are another example. These may be great for your own home, but the majority of residents will not take care of them.

• Don't Ignore Drainage Issues

I pay extra attention to where the water drains on and around my properties. Storm water drainage is a huge issue due to the amount of damage water can do to a house in a short amount of time. My area gets a lot of rain, so I am used to paying close attention to this. I have a list of houses that have had problems in the past or that I see have the potential to have problems when there are heavy storms. These houses get checked on after every major rain event with special attention paid to sensitive areas of concern. Simple things like a pile of leaves or other litter that diverts drainage water towards the house, disconnected rain gutter downspouts that playful kids have fooled with or a piece of plastic that clogs the driveway drain can cause water to get into the house. The few houses that I have with basements all have sump pumps that are checked on regularly. Because of this, I always have water damage on my mind whenever it rains.

. . .I always have water damage on my mind whenever it rains . . .

• **Don't Ignore The Site Structures – Retaining Walls Foundation Walls, And Slopes**
I learned the hard way how much maintenance that retaining walls and slopes can be. And speaking of maintenance, repairing an existing retaining wall can be very costly and time consuming. Most of the time these features were originally built before or at the same time as the other original foundation structures of the house. Now, after many years, it is leaning or cracked and broken so the repair is difficult. I make sure I have one of my grading contractors look at these situations before I get in too deep. Moving dirt can be fun but very expensive.

• **Don't Forget To Look Under The Hood Before You Buy**
Remember that old marketing saying, "you buy on emotion and justify with logic?" Well here is a good reminder to keep those emotions in check and do your due diligence. Check everything you can, look at everything you can and double-check yourself if you are getting excited about the deal at all. The fun part is the buy. The hard part is that after the purchase you will be married to this project, for better or worse, for a long time. The time to find out as much as you can about the house is before you write the check. I love buying houses with challenges that I can solve, but I do not enjoy being surprised by major problems that I didn't foresee.

. . . keep . . . emotions in check and do your due diligence . . .

• Don't Forget To Scrutinize Disclosures Carefully

I actually read all the disclosures required to be presented in closing documents now that they have become such a big issue. OK, I admit it. I really didn't pay any attention to all of the property disclosure forms when they first became a mandatory part of real estate transactions. Then I figured it was just another bunch of lawyers finding a way to make a living. Now I don't have a choice and I actually read them more carefully. The greatest challenge I have found is in the chain of title. I need to know what was disclosed to me so that I can be fair to the future buyers at some later date. This has an impact on how I will fill out my own disclosure forms when I sell.

• Don't Let a Home Inspector Go Alone

I don't care whether I'm buying or selling. I want to be on site when a home inspector is present. When I'm selling, I want to be there to see what he sees and have a chance to debate potential challenges. I learned the hard way, as usual, that once a home inspection report is written down, it's really hard to debate it. Sometimes there are logical reasons for things they are seeing, sometimes they speculate about what they think they see, and sometimes, there may no issue at all. I can tell you this though: Once their report is written, whatever is written becomes nearly immovable, almost as if a stone tablet has come down from a mountain issued by a supreme being.

. . . I want to be on site when a home inspector is present . . .

On the buying side of the equation, I will admit that I have paid for a home inspector once. This was on the last personal house my Princess and I purchased. This house is located on the waterfront, which I absolutely fell in love with. It has a tile roof, heat pump and a few other nice amenities that I was not very familiar with at the time. This combined with the fact that I was very emotionally involved, was the reason for hiring the inspector. I can't say as I learned anything unexpected, but it did assure me that I had covered my bases.

• Don't Buy A New Building Or Over-improved Building Hoping To Catch Up Somewhere Down The Line

I do not buy property that does not make sense today. If it doesn't make sense then I don't buy it. You are better off leaving your money in your mattress than putting yourself through all the stress a poor investment may cause. It has to make sense today in order for me to even consider it. I will not gamble on the future turning things around if that is the only thing that is going to "make sense" about the deal.

• Don't Be Tempted To Refinance To Pull Out Equity At The Expense Of Having The Property No Longer Make Sense

If there is anything that the current "economic crisis" has taught us or reminded us, it's not to pull equity out of your property as if the property were a piggy bank. It's so tempting because it's so easy to do. We really have to remember that there is a definite downside to giving ourselves a loan. I know this all too well as I have had experience with taking money out of good, solid properties in order to pursue other opportunities only to put the solid investment at risk. What can happen frequently does. . . and too frequently what does happen, isn't too pretty.

. . . pull(ing) . . .equity out of your property as if . . . (it's) a piggy bank (may put your) solid investment at risk . . .

Summing Up

Being successful in my particular model of real estate investment means paying close attention both to what I do and what I don't do. I've learned a lot about the real estate investment business as I practice it by virtue of having gone down so many alleyways, made so many mistakes, learned so many things, and had so many successes. I've packaged these kernels of learning in this chapter in such a way that corresponds to daily and sometimes strategic decision-making about key aspects of the business. These are general positions I take on the "global" level of this business.

In other books in my series I take a closer look at more detailed decisions, for those who would like to learn more about the finer scale of being engaged and developing this business on a daily, hourly, or minute-to-minute basis.

CHAPTER 8

My Business Model Is Providing High Quality Value Over A Long Period of Time, Optimizing My Options And Doing Well By Doing Good

I purchased this 4 bedroom, 1-bath house towards the end of 2001 for $75,000 and put another $13,000 into the initial rehabilitation. The rehabilitation included redoing the interior stairwell for nicer access to the upstairs bedroom and new exterior siding. This initial work and cleanup made it fit in with the rest of the neighborhood and it has been there ever since.

There is nothing particularly romantic or special about this house, its floor plan or location. As you can see by the picture, it is actually quite plain. I will tell you what makes this house so special to me: it fits my business plan to a T. The current residents are paying more than $1,000 a month in rent, are neat, clean, and have lived there for over seven years. I rarely hear from them and their inspections have always gone smoothly. This is one of those houses that I rarely think about because it never causes me a problem. I am no math wiz but I can tell you that any time I can invest less than $90,000 into a house and get a consistent $1,000 per month over a seven-year period. I will take it.

In This Chapter

In this chapter, I contrast the way most people approach real estate to the way I as a real estate investment professional approach real estate. There is a profound difference between these approaches that explains why I generate different results from others. You might also call this a summary of all the content in this book.

My Work – What Can be Called Value Investing In Real Estate Is All About Providing A High Quality Product

For most people, real estate is not an investment – it's a part time job. That job is usually maintenance and for the most part, maintenance is not a particularly welcome job – it's mainly thought of as a thankless chore. Even for most who consciously purchase real estate as an investment – they do so in a part time manner and regard a lot about what they do as kind of a joyless job that they engage in, mostly because of the promise of financial security that it promises to return.

I'm not that way. Real estate investment for me is a full-time occupation and it in no way resembles a part time job. Far from being joyless, I enjoy getting up every day and getting fully involved with it's challenges.

I realize, not many are like me, and I often wonder about this. On the other hand, I notice, not many enjoy the benefits that my chosen profession has provided for me – benefits I believe are a direct result of the investment I put into the business in commitment, time, and resources.

I believe, the greatest difference between the way I regard real estate investment and the way most others see it is in my attitude about the enterprise. I believe most see real estate investment as a means to an end – a money-making enterprise that leads to wealth. I don't see things that way. Don't get me wrong. I see nothing wrong with making money. On the other hand, I do see something very dysfunctional about trying to make money by focusing on making money. Real estate investment, in the manner that I have created, is all about providing a high quality product . . . a house that is truly a comfortable home for the residents whom I am privileged to serve. My attitude is that if I provide a good home for someone, everything else will fall into place. I'm not saying I can ignore everything else of whatever I'm providing. I'm just saying that providing a great house and the experience of living in it is the most important part – the highest priority element of the entire investment enterprise. At the same time as having a focus on product quality, I also see real estate investment as needing a long term, sustainable business and investment model. Without the latter, the former cannot be offered or continued.

. . . Real estate investment, in the manner that I have created, is all about providing a high quality product . . . a house that is truly a comfortable home for the residents whom I am privileged to serve . . .

I can better explain all of this by comparing what I do to other business enterprises where there is no question that product and service quality is memorable and the business is, has been, and will continue to be sustainable. Without naming names, I think all of us can think of outstanding, and most may say "classic" amusement parks, restaurants, computer products, movies, automobiles, clothing and a number of other products and services that really stand out as being the industry leaders. These are products and services that are defined by a combination of tangibles and intangibles that amount to the highest of standards – values or principles that define the product or service category they stand in.

. . . providing a great house and the experience of living in it is the most important part – the highest priority element of the entire investment enterprise . . .

Real estate investment, to me centers on developing and providing that high quality tangible and intangible standard of value to the real estate products and services I deliver – rental and renovated, resale housing for the housing consumer. The entire integrated process and all the related sub-processes of portfolio selection, purchase, renovation, renting, property management, property maintenance, long-term holding, and reselling is what I would call value investment.

To be more specific and describe it yet another way, I don't just invest dollars into a real estate venture. I invest everything I can think of to make it a high value standard that customers I cultivate (that I call residents and buyers, not residents) will want to live in for a very long time – the facilities, the property management, and the property maintenance all integrated together to form a unified package.

. . . The entire . . . process . . . the facilities, the property management, and the property maintenance all integrated together to form a unified package is what I would call svalue investment . . .

I also would describe real estate value investment from the investor's point of view as having a focus on the fundamentals of running a great business: providing great products and services in high demand, reliable income, desirable pre-tax and after-tax profit margins, excellent long term earnings, low debt, high free cash flow, low operating costs, easily manageable risks, and outstanding management – in short, an investment many investors would love to invest in.

. . . I also would describe real estate value investment from the investor's point of view as having a focus on the fundamentals of running a great business . . .

All together I would describe the entire package as doing well by doing good and doing right. I believe in offering high long-term value for fair long-term compensation. An important point needs clarification here. When I say high quality standards, I don't necessarily mean standards that are the highest priced or the highest cost. In fact, the prices and products I rent, renovate and resell are modest – prices that most average American homeowners could afford without a strain. This may sound impossible, but it probably sounds this way because real estate is one of the few areas where there can be a multiplicity of standards ranging from low cost to high cost. I'm not saying that higher-cost, higher priced values and services can't be provided either. I have chosen to keep my portfolio in the modest price range, but I'm certain that others may succeed at other higher standards and levels by following my methods.

. . . All together I would describe the entire package as doing well by doing good and doing right . . .

Understanding My Point Of View

Nearly everyone from the youngest of ages is connected with real estate as consumers through their homes either as renters or homeowners. When people purchase a home, they primarily make decisions to purchase based on consumer priorities such as proximity to work, school, floor plan, style, and paint colors, instead of investment factors such as floor plan functionality, roof longevity, and cost of maintenance. Later on, as these consumers become involved more as owners, their concerns change. Their modest levels of commitment when they initially move in are transformed to a more significant level of capital investment and time. The following are factors I consider when thinking of homes as investments:

• Long Term Rentals – Buying And Holding Property Until A Resident Buys It – As Long As That May Be
From the moment I purchase a house, I have the long term in mind. I have no interest in the latest get rich quick scheme that blows into town; and I have no interest in doing foolish, unethical business that will ruin my reputation. I like where I live and love what I do. I am all about having a product that is in demand now as a rental house with the ability to cash in that asset when I want to in the future. Long-term rentals are

my product of choice. Having happy, long-term residents are a great benefit during the rental period and in the end. I have sold many houses to existing residents. This is the ultimate win-win situation. They are the ones that inquire if I am willing to sell. They already know the house and have made it their home. The selling costs are minimal to me with no commissions or lost rent. This is a good deal.

. . . I have sold many houses to existing residents. This is the ultimate win-win situation . . .

- **Running Well Managed And Maintained Rental Properties While You Hold Them**

Setting up my rental houses in such a way as to make them easy to maintain is what gives me the options I'm looking for in a business. I can't afford to buy a house that does not fit into my program; I can't afford to have houses that are in disrepair; and I can't afford to have bad residents living in my houses. I run a business and I know that in order for my business to run efficiently, I have to have the correct systems in place. These systems are vital to my operation. I'm not the one you talk to at the cocktail party whining about my rentals and the terrible people that occupy them. To be blunt, I'm the opposite. I'm the guy that listens to their horror stories then often ends up buying their houses. This works for me! Running my business like a business and with a high quality product as my focus allows me to maintain a minimal level of emotional involvement. This is far different than most rental homeowners out there and far more effective.

. . . I run a business and . . . I have to have the correct systems in place . . .

- **Profiting In Seven Potential Ways:**
1. Buying Below Market

I buy houses at a below market prices or I don't buy at all. I don't believe in the theory of buying now and hoping the market will catch up later. I have to make money on the original purchase. Now purchasing houses using these criteria is a lot harder than buying anything that may just come along. I don't claim that it is always easy to find houses that make sense to purchase. I have had to implement numerous techniques over the years to accomplish this. Here is what I do claim: If the house does not make sense, then I don't buy it. It's as simple as that.

. . . I have to make money on the original purchase . . .

2.   Renovating To Add Value to Rent and Sales

When I look at a house to buy, I'm looking for how I will be able to use my skills to increase its value immediately. I need it to be worth more in sales value (for financing purposes and when I chose to sell it), capitalized value (should someone else choose to purchase and rent it) as well as rental value (generating more income). I accomplish this in several different ways. One of the most successful ways is by increasing the number of bedrooms. I find existing space within the structure to add bedrooms. Each of these bedrooms increases the rental value by ±$100 per month. This additional ±$100 a month makes one heck of a difference to my cash flow and in turn my overall sales and capitalized value.

. . . Each of these bedrooms increases the rental value by± $100 per month . . .

3.   Flip It, If Desired

The flip model is great as a potential option. The challenge comes when this is the only option. Look at all the people that got into buying and flipping houses based on the TV shows and get rich quick gurus that are now stuck with property that they have to come up with mortgage money to cover their negative cash flow. The right way to do a flip is when it is one of several options available to you and you choose to flip it. I am no newcomer to this idea. This is again one of those things I had to learn the hard way. I still have a couple of houses that I couldn't sell and had to rent out. These houses take down my overall cash flow of my business because they don't have positive cash flow. My equity position will be ok at some future date when the market heats up again, but for now, I have no choice but to suck it up and hold on.

. . . The right way to do a flip is when it is one of several options available to you and you choose to flip it . . .

4.   Rent To Capture Positive Cash Flow

Positive cash flow is awesome! No other words even begin to describe it. Here is the big kicker that most people will not share with you though. How much did that positive cash flow cost them? If you had to put 30-40% down to purchase a rental house so that it could generate a positive cash flow of ±$100 a month (over the cost of the mortgage, and operating and maintenance costs), is that really positive cash flow? I don't think so. This is why decreasing the purchase price and increasing the rental value is so important; and this is why your product – the house, is so important. I need a genuine positive cash flow -- one that takes into account my down payment because after renovating it to increase its sales value and rental income, I can get it back. How else can you keep going?

. . . I need a genuine positive cash flow . . .

5.   Rent For Tax Benefits

The tax benefits of owning real estate are tremendous. I am no expert in this field, but I have had the distinct advantage of having my father and our Chief Financial Officer carefully guide our business down the optimal tax path. The generous tax write-offs and depreciation really have been a benefit to our bottom line. I would suggest getting to know these advantages for yourself.

6.   Pull Out Equity In Refinances

Equity is only a hypothetical paper profit until you can use it. We just came out of a time in the financial world where accessing and withdrawing this equity was made a little too easy. Who in the world would refinance their rental houses and pull out the cash to invest in other ventures? Me. Guilty as charged! Now a few of the houses that had great positive cash flow for my business have a little less of it. When I consider the capitalization loss of this, I go to sleep wondering whether I did the right thing. Overall, we still have strong business fundamentals, but because I feel threatened by what we were able to do so easily, I think long and hard before pulling out equity now.

. . . I think long and hard before pulling out equity now . . .

7. Sell The House For Appreciation

Selling the house now or later is always an option that is available to me. I must confess that I'm not very good at it though. I really don't like to sell my rental properties. I sell other projects all the time that are designed and built to sell from the get-go, but the rentals are not. I have bought into the long-term hold philosophy and see the huge benefits for my business in it, so selling goes a little against my grain. The added value that I have created along the way in my houses, however, occasionally makes selling too good to pass up.

. . . I really don't like to sell my rental properties . . .

• It's Not About The Financing. It's All About The Product Quality And Associated Servicing

The acquisition financing may get me into the property, but the property itself is the product that must carry its weight in the marketplace. The product I produce must be in high demand and of a quality that will sustain itself over a long period of time. The servicing of this product is just as important, with ongoing maintenance and care given to it consistently.

Now I realize that this may be a lot different approach to this business than you may have heard about before; and I'm also aware that you may not have thought that renting property is a business and it deserves to be run like one. Well this is a business, as I see it – and a very good business at that – at least the way I think of it. This is a business that starts when you look at your first rental house to purchase. When this happens, a shift in your mindset has got to take place to assure your success whether you have two rentals or a hundred and two -- it doesn't matter. The financing is just one part of the equation -- not the product.

. . renting property is a business and deserves to be run like one .

• Quality Of Product

My houses are ultimately my products -- widgets so to speak. I have to produce widgets that I am proud of and feel good about. This is my nature. I cannot put lipstick on a pig and sell it as beautiful. It bothers me to the core when I encounter the countless, short-term thinkers in my industry --the ones that cover up problems in the house with a sheet of sheetrock and a new coat of paint. These same short-term thinkers are the ones that don't make it in the rental business because they don't think of the rental house as a product.

What do I mean that the house is a product? I mean it has to be safe, secure and able to be managed and maintained in an efficient manner. In my opinion, this may best be accomplished by looking at the house with the mindset that I will own it forever. How I set up the house and the systems within it (plumbing, electrical, floor plan, safety and others) for the long term benefit of both myself and my resident is vital to my operation.

. . . this may best be accomplished by looking at the house with the mindset that I will own it forever . . .

• Reliability of Income

Historically a good product is always in demand. My houses fit this description well and my vacancy rate reflects it. Reliability of income is in direct proportion to the vacancy rate. Having a house vacant, especially for any length of time, has a huge impact on cash flow. Having and maintaining a 4% vacancy rate, when the average for my county is at 7%

is a good measure of the quality of product I have. This tells me that I am providing an above average product that is in high demand.

. . . Having and maintaining a 4% vacancy rate, when the average for my county is at 7% is a good measure of the quality of product I have . . .

• **Owner's Equity**

When I purchase a house, I do so with the idea that I will need equity right away. I accomplish this by purchasing only those properties that I can substantially increase in value immediately. This immediate boost in equity assures me that the house will continue to make financial sense years down the road. Being able to gain access to this equity in times of need is also important. There's an old saying in the real estate world that says "you can't eat equity" -- which is to say no matter how much equity you may have, it's impossible to buy groceries with it while it's still sitting in the house.

. . . "you can't eat equity" . . .

Gaining access to the equity locked up in the house may be in the form of additional financing from traditional lenders or private individuals, in return for a certain amount of transaction cost. Having the equity accessible from the very beginning allows for this flexibility. It is important to look at cash flow when considering pulling money out of a rental house. Overleveraging an investment property (i.e., taking too much cash out) can be a very dangerous proposition. I have seen a lot of investors get themselves into trouble this way. I have been a little guilty of this a time or two myself. Spending and investment opportunities always seem to present themselves so the temptation is ever-present to access funds, wherever they may be to take advantage. The danger comes into play if some of those opportunities don't pan out quite the way you hope. If you take these funds out of your houses, you are then left with a house or two that does not have the level of cash flow it once had.

. . . Overleveraging an investment property . . . can be a very dangerous proposition . . .

• Competition

Amateur real estate investors continually screw things up. I'm sure this statement is true in any business, but it sure gets interesting at times. For example, the latest get rich quick scheme blows into town or a new TV show comes on that tells you how easy it is to make a fortune in real estate while in your pajamas. This has the effect of making sellers in my area nervous. They should be nervous. These "wanna-be" pitchmen that only have one way of being able to do things are not in a very good position to help out a potential seller. The odds of them creating a win-win situation are pretty slim.

Then there are the "out of towners". These are the ones that have come into my area and immediately start paying too much for properties. They see purchase prices considerably lower than where they came from, but do not realize that the market rents and appreciation rates are also lower. I wish they would just stay home. I welcome the few real competitors that are in my market. Competition keeps me sharp and I am not the only one in my area that is capable of buying or renting out houses.

. . . I welcome the few real competitors that are in my market . . .

• Profit Margins

Profit margins can be figured a lot of different ways and with numerous fancy equations. I like to keep things very simple. One way to measure my profit is to look at my return on additional investments in my houses. Let's take an example of a clean little updating remodel. I do these all the time on both new acquisitions and existing rental houses that I have. If I am looking at the updating to cost me -- say $15,000, then I have to see that I have gained at least $30,000 in increased equity. Now most of the time I can see a lot higher gain than that based on the type of renovations that I do, but I still use this as my simple equation. It provides me with a good check-and-balance rule-of-thumb type system.

. . . If I am looking at the updating to cost me – say $15,000, then I have to see that I have gained at least $30,000 in increased equity . . .

• **Free Cash Flow**
"Cash is King!" I don't know where my Father first heard those words but I know I have heard them from him many times over. Here is another meaning for the term -- you can't eat equity. What do both of these little gems mean? Cash flow is everything in this business. With it you can do anything. Without it you will suffer. Build your cash flow and you build your business, plain and simple. Houses that do not generate positive cash flow have no place in your portfolio.

. . . Cash flow is everything in this business. With it you can do anything. Without it you will suffer . . .

• **Debt**
Debt is something you have to get used to in my business and having debt is ok. There are different kinds of debt. Personal debt that the interest is not tax deductible is the worst kind to have. The debt that accompanies my business is the best kind to have. interest is tax deductible. Good debt is the kind that can be covered by the investment itself.

. . . in my business and having (the right kind of) debt . . . that can be covered by the investment itself . . . is ok . . .

• **Growing Population Demand**
It is no secret that our population is growing and with that the demand for housing. The economy fluctuates up and down but our population continues growing. I have always tried to be in a position to help this population have a place to call home and make a living in the process. Seems to be working so far.

. . . our population is growing and with that the demand for housing . . .

Finishing Up With These Thoughts

Many of my friends tell me that one of my greatest strengths is that I know my limitations. Upon reflection, I think they may be right. One reason I think so is that I'm absolutely certain that I'm not smart enough to engage in a lot of fancy footwork that I see so many others engaging in, in my chosen profession, but smart enough to make a profit without having to resort to gimmicks.

What kind of fancy footwork am I talking about? Well, I tell you what. I'll show you. I've compiled a list of approaches that I often wonder about, but haven't ever been "smart enough" to figure out. Here goes:

I'm Not Smart Enough . . .

- **I'm Not Smart Enough . . . To Be A Real Estate Market Timer**

. . . to buy at the lowest point in the real estate cycle or sell at the highest point in the real estate cycle. I can only guess when the market is at its highs and lows and definitely can't rely on those fluctuations to make a living. I actually much prefer a slow steady market to the great rise and falls we have seen lately.

- **I'm Not Smart Enough . . . To Be A Real Estate Speculator Or Day Trader**

. . . to dance in and out of markets and sidestep high transaction costs and financing terms. I see the flash in the pan guys that jump in and out of real estate markets all over the country, but that's not me. I have ventured into other areas before and usually ended up the worse for wear. I am now comfortable staying right in the market that I know and love. I have figured out that I can get into enough trouble right in my own back yard.

- **I'm Not Smart Enough . . . To Work On Small Margins And A High Number Of Transactions**

. . . to make money. I can't figure out how to make a living on skinny deals -- the kind that I have to hold my breath every time I pull up to the project during the remodel, hoping beyond hope that things were going much better that I knew they were. The skinny deals cause me to loose sleep too. A friend of mine has a saying that I try to live by. **"I can afford to pass up a good deal but I cannot afford to be in a bad deal."**

- **I'm Not Smart Enough . . . To Get Into High-Risk Propositions, for example . . .**

. . . to invest in high priced units in fashionable neighborhoods. I do not know how to make a long-term investment in areas in which the rent will not support the underlying mortgage. I can "flip" houses in higher end neighborhoods, but if I have to hold it for any length of time, my profit margin gets eaten up in interest and carrying costs. My conclusion is that this doesn't work for me. I have to be in the areas that will support themselves.

. . . I do not know how to make a long-term investment in areas in which the rent will not support the underlying mortgage . . .

- **I'm Not Smart Enough . . . To Get Into No Money Down, Short-Term Hard Money Loans And Fast Action, Money Turnover Schemes . . .**

. . . to earn a quick buck. I have borrowed money in about every way imaginable over the years, but scams have never been a part of any of them. I have a simple outlook on my business. It has to make sense to me how everyone involved is going to be ok. Win-win-win deals are all I am interested in.

. . . Win-win-win deals are all I am interested in . . .

• **I'm Not Smart Enough . . . To Plan Very Far In The Future Anticipating Every Challenge And Change In Consumer Tastes That Will Happen . . .**
. . . to know what will happen before it happens. I don't know what fad will be coming into town next, but I do know how to keep my product basic and appealing to the masses. This approach is the only one that makes sense to me.

. . . I do know how to keep my product basic and appealing to the masses . . .

• **I'm Not Smart Enough . . . To Know Which Guru-Du-Jour Scheme To Follow To Get Rich Quick On . . .**
. . . to support my money making habits. Let's face facts again here for a moment. My industry is full of get rich quick scam artists that leave a wake of disappointed people behind them. In my experience, the majority of these fast talkers start out with a couple of pretty good ideas but get all caught up in the "fantasy" that they think people want to hear. I know the truth. You know the truth. Odds are your parents and grandparents told you the truth. There is no "get rich quick" scheme available to anyone that has a conscience. Real estate is essentially just hard work that happens to be very rewarding.

. . . My industry is full of get rich quick scam artists that leave a wake of disappointed people behind them . . .

• **I'm Not Smart Enough . . . To Know Alchemy, Turning Something Worthless Into Gold . . .**
. . . to fulfill the many things on my wish lists. I am not smart enough to fix everything that I come across. Some projects are just not going to work for me. I have taken on a lot of different projects with the main motivating factor being that it would be a new experience but I have also passed on numerous other ones. It has to have the basic pieces in place in order to get it to where I need it to go.

. . . (I accept that) . . . some projects are just not going to work for me . . .

• **I'm Not Smart Enough . . . To Know Which Hedge Fund, Credit Default Swap, and Tax Shelter Technique Works Best And Lowers My Risk . . .**
. . . to sidestep the basic expenses of doing business. In this day and age, there are a lot of funny things going on with the economy. Unfortunately scam artists are not unique to the real estate industry and everyone has to be cautious about whose advice they follow. The latest and greatest ways to get out of your debt or avoid paying any taxes is not the way to build a long-term business. I am not interested in anything that requires me to hang my head in shame in my own hometown.

. . . The latest and greatest ways to get out of your debt or avoid paying any taxes is not the way to build a long-term business . . .

• **I'm Not Smart Enough . . . To Guess What Will Be Fashionable And In High Demand Each Selling Season . . .**
. . . to get the upper hand on the competition. Normal sells. I believe in this and have proved it to myself time and time again. I have tried to be fashionable and put the latest and greatest trendy things into my houses, but it usually just does not pan out in the long run. I paid a lot more attention to the trends when I was building new homes for sale than I do now. I keep up on trends as it is in my curious nature to do so, but I do not study the latest and greatest as I used to. In my rental market, safety, cleanliness and basic normal (for lack of a better description) outlasts fashionable all day long.

. . . the latest and greatest trendy things in my houses . . . usually just does not pan out . . .

- **I'm Not Smart Enough . . . To Know What Hot-Shot Management Specialist To Hire To Run My Company Better Than I Can . . .**

. . . to boost my profits quicker. My team and I are the best for my operation. We have survived many ups and downs together and have always come through fine. We are just as I said -- a team and one that I would not trade for anything. I need this team around me to be as dedicated to our product as I am. I cannot achieve that by hiring an outsider to come in and run things.

Okay, now you know my limitations and why I stay within their boundaries. On the other side of this are my capabilities. Not only do my friends say that I know my limitations, but I also know my capabilities. Thus I'd like to give you a sense of what I'm smart enough to know.

On the Other Hand, I Have Learned Enough . . .

- **I Have Learned Enough . . . To Know That I Have A Business Model That Works Really Well . . .**

. . . to do amazing things. Through many years of trials and tribulations I can tell you that this business model works like a charm. I have done it enough to know that I will never have it perfect, but whenever I stray from it, I'm usually heading for trouble. Investment homes and their residents are both a very valuable asset when treated right. Want to know how I know this business model works . . . because we concocted it from many real life experiences of our own.

. . . Through many years of trials and tribulations I can tell you that this business model works like a charm . . .

When my Dad, our current COO and myself got together and started building our rental portfolio seriously, we did not necessarily start from scratch. Dad had a couple of rental properties at the time and I had a lot of construction experience. The addition of the "third leg of our stool" brought in the necessary management skills to run an ongoing operation.

Throughout the first couple of years, there was a lot of trial and error going on in all of our departments. Dad was responsible for the financing leg and had to have the foresight and means to keep everything going. Financing was and still is something he managed well and is extremely good at. The management systems had to be set up along the way. I had to learn how to best prepare a house to rent and maintain over a long period of time instead of selling right away. Boy did I make my share of mistakes! For most everything I currently do now, the odds are I can tell you a reason why it is done that way from a hard lesson I learned from personal experience -- episodes that more often than not cost me money. Those are the easiest to remember. So our "trial and terror" method of growing our business is not the way others should have to do it. That is why I am here. I can help.

. . . our "trial and terror" method of growing our business is not the way others should have to do it. That is why I am here. I can help . . .

• I Have Learned Enough . . . To Know That I Can Do My Business Successfully Over And Over Again . . .
. . . to perfection. I know for a fact that I do not have a top-secret formula here. I also know that my business model is not unique to my area. People need housing and they want to be respected and treated right. On the other side of the coin are the sellers of the investment houses I purchase. Believe it or not, the sellers want the same thing. It is human nature to want to do something that makes us feel good. I have purchased several houses from sellers who have told me that they felt good about what it was I was going to do with their house. They added that this is why they agreed to my price and terms. This business model may be tweaked a bit here and there, the numbers adjusted to fit particular situations, and general modifications made, but the bottom line is that it will work in working class neighborhoods all over the world. There is no doubt in my mind that this is true.

. . . This business model . . . will work in working class neighborhoods all over the world . . .

- **I Have Learned Enough . . . To Know That I Can Have Long-Term Predictable, Profitable Results . . .**

I have always looked at my business as a long-term investment. I must admit that when I started, I was relying on faith and the wisdom of my father to keep me going at times. When you are working tirelessly for future benefits, on occasion, it can be hard to keep going. Now I can see the value in what we started many years ago and it is awesome. . .

- **I Have Learned Enough . . . To Know That Conditions Change In My Market All The Time . . .**

My father has always told me that in business the only thing for sure is that things will be different. This statement has been so true so many times. Property sellers have different attitudes depending on the local economic conditions they face. Now as I say this I am compelled to emphasize that although their attitudes change with changing times, their needs remain very much the same. By this I mean there are people that always need to sell, other people that need to buy and still other people that need to rent. These basics don't change and the better I have come to understand this, the better I have become at this whole game -- a game that is ever changing and an awful lot of fun.

. . . (This is) a game that is ever changing and an awful lot of fun . . .

- **I Have Learned Enough . . . To Know That Acquisition Techniques Change All The Time And That's Why I Go . . .**

. . . to the gurus that I do. Along with the ever-changing attitudes of sellers come new acquisition techniques. I pay close attention to all of these whether I agree with them or not. I have learned a lot from many of the real estate teachers that have come before me and will continue to seek out more learning opportunities. It may surprise you to know that I also keep up on quite a few of the so-called "guru's" that I do not care for as well. My philosophy has always been that I need to know as much as I can about what is going on in my market -- the good, the bad and the ugly is all a part of that. I have to know what the people I am dealing with have been hearing and reading in order to better understand their current attitudes. Once I know this, I can better help them meet their needs and that is what this whole game is about. Helping people get what they want.

. . . I need to know as much as I can about what is going on in my market . . .

- **I Have Learned Enough . . . To Know That I Don't Know Everything . . .**
. . . to know that there is more to know. I know that when I was younger, I may have been accused of thinking that I knew everything, but the years have worn on me. I have the scars to guide me now. Now I'm fully aware that I'm forever on a journey of learning -- a journey that I most enjoy and one that will go on all of my days. The world has a way of humbling the small businessman along the way, and especially this one.

- **I Have Learned Enough . . . To Know What I Know And Just Enough Of What I Don't Know . . .**
. . . to know that I need to keep learning.   Wasn't it Popeye who said "I am what I am and that's all that I am"? Well I think he was a pretty smart guy. I know how to do what I do. I have worked with my team for years to develop the system that we now have. I know how to coach and guide people that are on their way to success in a similar fashion. I am very comfortable in what I do know, how to handle the things that I do not know, and how to tell people that I don't even know what I don't know. One thing I do not know how to do is to cheat people out of their hard earned money. No deal is worth sacrificing my integrity or those of my team.

• I Have Learned Enough . . . To Know What I Can Do Myself, What I Need Help With And . . .

. . . to be humble enough to admit what needs working on. My father's outlook on continuing education in all forms has served me very well. Together we have paid many thousands of dollars to numerous coaches, consultants and experts in many different fields over the years. Hiring the right people, coaches if you will, to help us get to where we have wanted to go has been instrumental in our success. Having an experienced coach on your team to guide you to the next level is one of the smartest decisions you will make and some of the best money you can spend.

. . . Hiring the right people . . . coaches . . .to help us get to where we have wanted to go has been instrumental in our success . . .

• I Have Learned Enough . . . To Know How To Find The Right Help. I'm A Good Quarterback. I Know Where . . .

. . . to go and what to do. Finding the appropriate and experienced experts to help guide me along the way is a job in itself at times. Networking and always having an open mind has been my way of approaching this. I have always enjoyed learning and find that most people are very helpful when given a chance.

• I Have Learned Enough . . . To Know That Problems And Challenges Will Happen On A Regular Basis . . .

. . . to know I will handle them calmly without calamity resulting. Staying calm in the face of a storm and being able to resolve problems successfully at the same time is more of an art than anything else. I have never enjoyed being around people that yell and scream or otherwise become out of control under stress. Things happen everyday that are unforeseen. Challenges arise from projects themselves or the people that are involved. I have to stay calm keep my eye on the problem at hand and lead my team through this maze of challenges on an ongoing basis. This is the only way I know how to do it.

. . . Things happen everyday that are unforeseen . . .

• I Have Learned Enough . . . To Know That The House Is My Most Important Product . . .

. . . and what I mean is my approach to improving it, maintaining it, and giving very special treatment to all those great residents who live within it's boundaries. I have a different outlook on what I do than most anybody else I have met in this business. The house is my product and its resident is my customer. I don't allow anyone associated with my business to refer to our customers as "residents". I believe its negative connotation diminishes the importance of them. I pride myself in producing a product that both its resident and I can be proud of. This establishes a mutually beneficial relationship that can be sustained for years.

. . . I pride myself in producing a product that both its resident and I can be proud of . . .

• I Have Learned Enough . . . To Know That I Know How To Produce My Product and Optimize It . . .

. . . in my marketplace. I know what works in my marketplace; I know the areas that I will invest in; I know what to produce in those areas. I know how many bedrooms is optimum and what other amenities my residents require. I also know how to look at other markets to determine where I should invest. This is much more than just a selection of a location but also determining what to produce to best fit in the market.

. . . I know what works in my marketplace . . .

• I Have Learned Enough . . . To Know How To Set Up Systems, Put Them In Place And Manage Them . . .

. . . to keep everything going. I have learned a lot through E-myth and their coaching program about systems and their correct development. I highly recommend that you get their books and absorb the information like a sponge. Under their guidance, my team and I were able to set up the systems needed to efficiently run our business. Going through this process was an enormous project for us -- a project that would have been a lot easier had we started it earlier on. Instead we waited until we were at a company size where everyone involved was running around like chickens with our heads cut off. Please don't do this to yourself. Setting up the systems to run my business has been one of the best things I have ever done.

. . . Setting up the systems to run my business has been one of the best things I have ever done . . .

• I Have Learned Enough . . . To Know What Deals To Walk Away From . . .

. . . to avoid disaster. At this stage of my career, I'm very confident in knowing that I have to focus my time, energy and money on the best deals possible. A marginal or skinny deal will take as much, if not more resources than a good deal, so why bother with it in the first place. A bad deal is a disaster in all areas. The bad deal will not only deplete your resources, but have a negative effect on your attitude as well. As my friend so eloquently told me years ago "you can afford to pass up a good deal but you cannot afford to get into a bad deal." I also know that I cannot do every deal that is out there nor should I want to.

. . . I'm very confident in knowing that I have to focus my time, energy and money on the best deals possible . . .

• I Have Learned Enough . . . To Know That I Can Afford To Pass On A Good Deal But I Can't Afford to Be In A Bad Deal . . .

. . . because it's possible that it may only take one bad deal to ruin the business. Dad drummed this idea into my head again and again over the years. It's a conservative point of view and a point of view that underscores the importance to doing as much due diligence as is reasonably possible to do to dispel as many of the unknowns in a deal as possible. Though it's not possible to have "perfect" knowledge, it is possible to make good educated guesses based on competent and affordable information. A bad deal drains not only my resources but my energies as well. Real estate deals do not go perfectly as planned and my experience has taught me that they rarely get better than they first looked. My ego has gotten in the way of this in the past with me thinking that I can fix anything out there in the market, but I have been stung time and again. If it doesn't feel right, has too many things that would have to go perfect in order for it to make sense, etc… I am a lot better off passing and going on to the next deal.

I'm currently experiencing just such a situation. At the time of negotiating a recent home sale, I experienced a person who was very difficult to please. It just seemed that at every turn, he was making things more and more difficult to resolve issues. My intuition and my staff kept telling me that he was going to be a real problem to deal with. The problem was we needed to close this sale because we had determined that we were better off selling the unit he purchased than holding on. The bottom line was that we went through with the sale knowing this purchaser may be a problem going down the road, but hoping that he wouldn't be. Then guess what? He turned out to be as bad and probably even worse than we thought he would be. With 20-20 hindsight, I now see that as much as we needed that sale, it would have probably been better walking away from it.

. . . a bad deal drains . . . resources (and) energy . . .

• I Have Learned Enough . . . To Know That I Need To Constantly Learn As Much As I Possibly Can About My Business . . .

. . . to keep on top of a constantly changing world. I enjoy learning about my business and many other things. I think of learning as a way of life and not final destination. My father has told me since I was young that education, like life, is a journey. I guess I bought into that theory of his also.

. . . I think of learning as a way of life . . .

• I Have Learned Enough . . . To Know That I Need To Constantly Develop My Resources . . .

. . . to sharpen my "tools" so I can use them when I need them. Consistently developing my resources has been essential to my success. Networking in my local real estate groups and associations has been a part of my life for well over 15 years. It needs to be a part of yours. These local associations are the lifeblood of this business. The people in attendance are the ones out there doing business everyday. These same people are, for the most part, very informative and helpful to seasoned and new investors alike. Along with that most of them regularly have guest speakers that cover many educational topics. I have learned over the years that I can learn a little something from most all of these speakers. Granted, some more than others but it is always informative. As I now move more into the speaking realm I look forward to being the one that is passing along some valuable knowledge to those in attendance.

. . . Networking in my local real estate groups and associations has been a part of my life for well over 15 years. It needs to be a part of yours . . .

• I Have Learned Enough . . . To Know That I Need To Do Due Diligence . . .

. . . to trust but verify, as Ronald Reagan counseled all those who would listen about competent management.   I need to take every potential project through the system that I have established. This is the only way to make sure that it will fit into my business. There is no way to short cut this process. The risk of not doing my due diligence is too great.

• I Have Learned Enough . . . To Know That No House Is Going To Be Perfect In Design, Execution And Maintenance For Its Residents . . .

. . . to create the perfect experience. I know that I cannot make any house perfect. No house is perfect, nor any of my investment houses or my personal home. I do the best I can with what I have to work with and go from there.

. . . I do the best I can with what I have to work with and go from there . . .

Summing Up

I have earned a very good living at practicing value investing in real estate. This is not fast money, easy money, or killer money as some people practice real estate investment. Value investing in real estate is all about creating, maintaining, and sustaining a very high quality product – namely rental and permanent housing for ordinary people and building a genuine business for the serious investor where value is produced and delivered for a fair return. This is what I mean when I ask the question, "Why isn't it all about the house?"

. . . Value investing in real estate is all about creating, maintaining, and sustaining a very high quality product – namely rental and permanent housing . . .

The business model I follow should not be, but probably is kind of an anomaly in real estate investment circles in that only a relatively small proportion of investors are practicing it relative to the number of real estate investors that exist. While the requirements for operating my business model are not easy to fulfill, they aren't outrageous, nor do they depend upon heroic, unrealistic, or unreachable assumptions. All the stars in the heavens do not need to be lined up just perfectly to produce a great return on investment as some real estate investment models seem to depend upon, for example the quick flip. On the contrary, ordinarily intelligent, diligent people can fulfill my business model in many locations and in most parts of the business cycle. There are built in to my model so many alternative ways of earning income that it can succeed no matter what part of the real estate or business cycle we find ourselves in. I need as many of these ways to make income as possible on each and every property I have because there are also many things that can go wrong. There are countless possible pitfalls and disasters that can happen when you start buying properties, and these can come at you from many directions -- construction problems, resident issues and challenges created by the municipalities, just to name a few. This business is not without risk, but those risks can be mitigated with the proper education, experience and professional help.

... ordinarily intelligent, diligent people can fulfill my business model in many locations and in most parts of the business cycle ...

There is nothing I would like better than to see real estate investment become an ordinary good business practice, instead of the "gold rush" mentality that many seem to associate with it. I've attempted to show you that not only can this approach be feasible, but also it can be potentially very lucrative. Frankly, having fewer speculators around to foul up the real estate market and the political regulatory environment in pursuit of elusive get rich quick schemes would make my day.

... There is nothing I would like better than to see real estate investment become an ordinary good business practice ...

SUMMARY

Look at this house. Does it get any better than this? Doesn't the white picket fence and welcoming entry have you expecting Beaver Cleaver's mom June to be waiting for your arrival with newspaper and slippers in hand? This house has it all: a comfortable interior layout of three bedrooms and one bath, fireplace, attached garage, hardwood floors, tasteful wood trim throughout the house that adds to its coziness, and a private fully fenced backyard perfect for summer Bar-B-Q's. This is what I strive for -- my house, my skill and my hard work contributing to a good, solid neighborhood; my house being able to be someone's home; and my investment becoming a family's pride and joy.

That's it in a nutshell for me. This is what I am all about. I restore the existing housing stock, making it possible for the social structure of our communities to thrive. I have single handedly changed neighborhoods for the better by establishing new standards. I've done this because it was the right thing to do. I thoroughly enjoy what I do and I care about my community. I can't be any other way. I will not succumb to the temptation and greed of the slumlord. I will not go in and out of markets like the flippers, not caring what challenges I leave for the next guy. I want all my houses to look just like the one pictured here. I want to smell the homemade cookies being baked in the oven and the families playing in the yard.

Wrapping Up

I'm the CEO and part owner of a real estate investment enterprise that has achieved sustainable real estate success over a 15-year period by virtue of having a remarkably robust and effective business model.

I'm sharing this model with you the reader and the world as described in this book and other forums, in part, to encourage its wider use. I'm convinced that doing so will provide guidance that will be found to be sorely needed when it is discovered how well it works, for this model is a description of almost certain financial and community success wherever it can be applied. It stands in stark contrast to the recent meltdown in the real estate industry that fills our daily news media and has been filling it for the past year with tales of woe.

. . . this model is a description of almost certain financial and community success wherever it can be applied . . .

The recent demise of the real estate industry has shocked, disappointed and upset me for I know that despite what many critics are fond of saying, it didn't and doesn't need to be this way. How can it be when for so many years, my largely invisible real estate investment business has been quietly producing great products that are in high demand and at the same time generous returns for me?

It's been a significant surprise to me that more folks don't do what I do and my company has done in our industry, because if they did, and the real estate industry and even government regulation were built around what we do and have done, things would be different. Is that too boastful a statement? I hope not. It wasn't intended to be. I think it's a simple statement of fact. In our little corner of the world, I've found that people embrace with open arms what they can see and understand of our approach. The long time residents of our rental homes are by and large very pleased with our products and services as can be seen by the many friends and family of the residents who they have referred to us. Our community and those we work with are also very pleased with who we are and what we do. Our business provides a valuable community service that is in high demand. Our lower than average vacancy rates are testimony to that.

. . . It's been a significant surprise to me that more folks don't do what I do and my company has done in our industry . . .

My company and especially me don't share our successful approach with you in this book out of a sense of altruistic "do-goodism". On the contrary, I do it because I am sick of seeing what is clearly an unbalanced overrepresentation in the marketplace of scam-artists, snake-oil salesmen, and pretenders of many different stripes on the seminar circuit, on television, and in other media. I know the false dreams and tales they spin are not what they claim to be because I know from many years of personal experience in this industry what works and what doesn't. I want to show people in our industry and the wider world what a good business real estate investment as I practice it can be for the community at large and business people in particular by showing you what I've done from my own personal experience. This is not and need not be a get rich quick scheme for quick buck artists, liars, and cheats.

In this book I have laid out our overall business model for all to see. I take a long-term view. I am in this business as a business and in business for a time horizon as far as the eye can see. I take a simple approach characterized by the purchase of property using standard methods; followed by a renewal process of recycling worn out, obsolete rental housing properties for ordinary folks; followed by a process of selecting qualified residents for long term rental of these properties; followed by a long-term management and maintenance process of holding on to the property; and completed by the sale of the property to the long-term resident of the property or some other financially qualified person in a normal way, at an unpressured time with reasonable and realistic terms where everyone wins.

My approach is simple, but it isn't easy. I take the challenge seriously and apply my best efforts. Unlike many who provide what I do, I apply myself to the work full time. I take great pains to do this business right using highly skilled managers, extraordinary vigilance, effective management systems, continuous improvement, resourcefulness, and creativity.

. . . My approach is simple, but it isn't easy . . .

I am very proud to present the product of 15 years of pains taking trial and error to you. If you seriously follow the approach I've outlined here and in several other books I am writing on this subject to come, you will taste the sweet success and personal satisfaction I have received in this industry. My personal involvement in this industry has created a very nice life for me and my family of seven . . . that has paid and will continue paying dividends to my community, my fellow workers and me far into the future. If you decide to join me on the same path, I hope to meet you sometime in the near future. I invite you to share your success stories with me.

. . . If you seriously follow the approach I've outlined here . . . you will taste the sweet success and personal satisfaction I have received in this industry . . .

G L O S S A R Y

....

"All In The Real Estate Investment Business" — It is full-time in the sense that it is almost always on my mind or not far from being on my mind even though I don't spend a lot of time at my office. I devote all of my professional energy to it. I've invested not only a lot of money that I have earned and put right back in to the business, but also a lot of time – much of which goes unaccounted for (meaning I don't watch it all that carefully. I just do what I find necessary to be done). All that being said, I still have a good, balanced life in and away from real estate. Have I mentioned that I am very happily married; have a beautiful family of five children; have a beautiful home; am an avid fisherman; and also have a charter boat business? I have a lot of friends whom I spend time with and there is a lot of laughter in my home. I believe that I have achieved a very happy balance in my life.

Boring Business — all parts of the business are so well organized, so efficiently operated, and so systemized (advertising, administration, maintenance, replacement, customer service, revenue collections, sales, purchases, renovations, property management) that they require minimal effort and waste to operate

Free Cash Flows — unburdened cash flows available to be spent on anything a business requires

Flipped Out — the unsustainable practice of purchasing real estate property, then being unable to quickly turn around sell it for a profit. In my opinion this is not a real business. Flipping is destructive to the real estate business, ruinous of our communities and destabilizing of our nation.

Full Immersion Serious Money Making Business — my business of growing, developing, and managing real estate investment property on a full time basis

Garbage is My Life — the real view from the inside of the rental home investment business as distinguished from the fantasy view

Good Debt — the kind of debt that can be covered by the investment itself

High Demand Product — a "must have". With this in mind, the business is probably fulfilling fundamental human needs: food, shelter or clothing -- needs that are never-ending, no-matter-what, no-matter how, no-matter-who

High Relative Liquidity — the ability to sell off assets quickly, if and when desired

I Don't Buy Homes — that have been in a fire; I don't buy homes that are in scary neighborhoods where there are drug dealers; and I don't buy homes that I can't purchase for a low enough price to repair and create positive cash flow.

Immediate and Long Term Selling Options — the ability to:
- purchase and sell
- fully renovate and sell
- fully renovate and rent
- purchase, partially renovate, and sell
- sell on option
- purchase, trade, and exchange

Multiple Investment Opportunities — my business can be reliably profitable year in, year out, whether the market is going up, going down, going sideways, going backwards, going upside down, going inside out by appreciation, depreciation tax advantages, flipping, holding on, buying low then selling high, renting, optioning, trading, renovating, building new, attaching, detaching, subdividing, smart long term maintenance, property managing

Negative Cash Flow — when the investor has to come up with extra cash to pay for what is not covered by rental income of a house including the carrying cost of the home (monthly mortgage + ongoing property management fees + annual maintenance costs) – the opposite of positive cash flow

Organic Acquisition — landlords who rent property by default, being unable to sell property due to unfavorable market conditions

Overleveraging an Investment Property — taking too much equity or cash out of a home

Passive Residual Income — a business that is earning money when you're not on the job – when you are sleeping, on vacation, and involved in your hobbies

Personal Debt — debt where interest is not tax deductible

Positive Cash Flow — after renovation, the amount you are receiving in rent completely pays for the carrying cost of the home (monthly mortgage + ongoing property management fees + annual maintenance costs).

Preferred Amount of Renovation — judgment call by a renovation expert

Preferred Condition of Property to Invest In — judgment call by a renovation expert

Preferred Kind of Neighborhood to Invest in — starter homes

Preferred Kind of Property to Acquire — single family

Preferred Price to Pay for Investment Property — below market

Real Estate Investment As a Business — I'm in it to earn a good living at it –a full-time living using a robust (likely to generate significant income I can comfortably support myself and my family with), seasoned (tested over time), and sustainable (able to be engaged in again and again) business model

Real Estate Investment For Life — for the long-term -- way beyond three months or even one year -- I've been in my version of the real estate investment business for 15 years already and I'm just getting warmed up!

Real Estate Market Timer — buying real estate at the lowest point in the real estate pricing cycle or sell at the highest point in the real estate pricing cycle

Real Estate Value Investing — what I call providing long term, basic housing for people to live in so that they can go about their lives feeling secure, stable and focused on the parts of their lives that are most important to them while giving myself many options to earn income.

Reliably Profitable Year-In, Year-Out — my business that is organized on a long term basis – basically buying and holding, establishing, building, and reliably maintaining stable residential communities for the benefit of all concerned

Renters — people who occupy my homes that some call tenants and I prefer to call residents

Rental Renovation — renovation primarily for the purpose of rental (as distinguished from sales renovations that are intended for making positive short-term impressions)

Residents — renters that some call tenants, but I think is demeaning so I call them residents

Significant Renovation — renovation intended to increase rental revenue (for example by adding more bedrooms) as distinguished from cosmetic renovation.

Skinny Deals — real estate transactions that depend upon small profit margins and a high number of transactions

Socially Beneficial — my business provides an important social benefit

Sustainable — able to keep the business up or keep going with a reasonable amount of business effort, no heroics, no herculean assumptions, and no excessive risk

Sustainability —
- year round all-weather, all-season success
- products that are always in demand -- housing
- products that fulfill simple, classic needs -- shelter

Residents — renters or tenants that I prefer to call residents

Ugly Ducklings — modest homes – by which I mean under-designed for the neighborhood, smaller than normal, or in run-down condition

What Is Real Estate Investor? — having both the right personality characteristics to handle the requirements, stresses, and challenges of the job and the right business model structure to earn your keep

What Is Real Estate Investment? — there exists a full-time (or greater than part-time) real estate investment business model that works and works very well

When To Sell Properties? —
- immediately after renovation - rarely
- to rid ourselves of unanticipated low quality properties
- when one of our residents wants to buy
- when we need the money - rarely
- when we reach a high point in the appreciation cycle
- when one or more of the positive cash flow factors changes
- when there is a forced sale by government

Work Flow Systems — systems of organization of our operations from emyth systems that organize our operating goals and administration to our streamlined customer service operations, to our property management and property maintenance systems that keep our operations streamlined and efficient

REFERENCES

1. American Housing Survey (AHS), March 18, 2009 National 2007 American Housing Survey for the United States in 2007, Series H-150 (Census 2000-based-weighting tables), Bureau of the Census, Economics and Statistics Administration, U.S. Department of Commerce, Washington, D.C. , accessible at www.census.gov/ hhes/www/housing/ahs/nationaldata.html

2. Current Housing Reports, Housing and Household Economic Statistics, Property Owners and Managers Survey, Census Bureau, October 1998, U.S. Department of Commerce, Economic and Statistics Administration.

3. Individual Landlord Survey Final Report, July 5, 2005, Housing Affordability and Finance Series, Canadian Mortgage and Housing Corporation (CMHC)

4. San Francisco Property Owners Survey Summary Report, August 2003, Study Moderator: Joe Grubb, San Francisco Board of Supervisors, Bay Area Economics

T E L L   U S   W H A T   Y O U   T H I N K

As the reader of this book, you are the most important critic and commentator. We value your opinion and want to know what we are doing right, what we could do better, in what areas you would like to see us publish, and any other words of wisdom that you are willing to pass our way.

When you contact us, please be sure to include this book's title, ISBN, and author, as well as your name and e-mail address. We will carefully review your comments and share them with the author and editors who worked on this book.

E-mail: Mike@SandersonInc.com

A B O U T   T H E   A U T H O R

Mike Sanderson is the CEO of a family business that owns, manages and maintains over 100 revenue producing rental units – a majority being single-family residences that were purchased in disrepair. Mike has actively participated at all levels of the purchase, constructin and remodeling of over 100 homes and 20+ multiple unit buildings. He has numerous years in the construction of roads, new homes and remodeling that give him the distinct advantage of having a vast amount of experience.

- First home at 19 years old was a 1960 10X50 mobile home. He now lives on the water in beautiful Puget Sound
- He has actively participated at all levels of the construction and remodel of over 100 homes and 20+ multiple unit buildings
- He has numerous years in the construction of roads, new homes and remodeling that give him the distinct advantage of having a vast amount experience
- Past Builders Council Chairman, Master Builders Association of Pierce County
- Past Board of Directors, Master Builders Association of Pierce County
- Past State Board of Directors, Building Industry Association of Washington
- Washington State Remodeling Excellence Award Winner-Whole house remodel division
- Certified Manufactured Home Installer, Washington State
- Vested in the Operating Engineers Union Local #612
- Countless Real Estate and Construction seminars and classes since he was 17 years old
- United States Coast Guard 100 Ton Captains License

WORK HISTORY

1983-1985 **Sandco Properties/Self Employed**
Washington and Alaska
Remodeling and New Construction of single
family residences and multi unit properties

1984-1988 **Washington State Real Estate License**

1985-1993 **Tucci and Sons/Job Foreman**
Tacoma, Washington
Heavy highway construction

1993-2000 **Reflection Homes/Self Employed**
Tacoma, Washington
President
New Construction homes, built and sold, land
development and remodeling

2000-Present **Sandco Properties/Self Employed**
Tacoma, Washington
CEO

1993-Present **Various land development and new
construction projects as part owner, both
residential and commercial.**
Responsible for design, permits and construction

Contact Information:

Mike Sanderson
PO BOX 111821
TACOMA WA 98411

Email: Mike@SandersonInc.com

WHAT A REAL ESTATE BUSINESS LOOKS LIKE

#1   3 bedroom / 1 bath
1,042 square feet
Built 1937
Status: was A, now A

#2   3 bedroom / 1 bath
1,280 square feet
Built 1922
Status: was A, now A

#3   3 bedroom / 1 bath
922 square feet
Built 1890
Status: was B, sold as C

#4   4 bedroom / 2 bath
1,431 square feet
Built 1978
Status: was B, sold as C

#5   3 bedroom / 1 bath
972 square feet
Built 1925
Status: was B, now B

#6   3 bedroom / 1 bath
932 square feet
Built 1968
Status: was C, now A

#7   3 bedroom / 1 bath
1,083 square feet
Built 1942
Status: was C, now B

#8 5 bedroom / 1 3/4 bath
1,450 square feet
Built 1910
Status: was C, now B

#9 (2) 1 bedroom / 1 bath
apartments plus Main
Office
500 square feet per unit
Built 1907
Status: was C, now A

#10 4 bedroom / 3 bath
2,550 square feet
Built 1944
Status: was B, sold as A

#11 5 bedroom / 2 ½ bath
2,232 square feet
Built 1912
Status: was C, now B

#12 3 bedroom / 1 ½ bath
2,800 square feet
Built 1937
Status: was B, sold as A

#13 (12) 1 bedroom / 1 bath
Apartments
500 square feet per unit
Built 1972
Status: was D, now C+

#14 3 bedroom / 2 bath
1971 square feet
Built 1919
Status: was C, now B

#15 6 bedroom / 2 ¾ bath
2,800 square feet
Built 1959
Status: was C, sold as A

#16   3 bedroom / 1 bath
964 square feet
Built 1943
Status: was C, now B+

#17   3 bedroom / 1 bath
832 square feet
Built 1925
Status: was C, now B+

#18   3 bedroom / 1 bath
1,032 square feet
Built 1943
Status: was C, now B

#19   2 bedroom / 1 bath
884 square feet
Built 1910
Status: was D, now C+

Flipped Out?

#20   3 bedroom / 2 ½ bath
1,557 square feet
Built 2007
Status: was B+, now B+

#21   3 bedroom / 1 bath
1,022 square feet
Built 1960
Status: was C-, now C+

#22   4 bedroom / 1 bath
1,293 square feet
Built in 1950
Status: was C+, now B+

#23   2 bedroom / 1 bath
925 square feet
Built in 1905
Status: was C, now B

#24   3 bedroom / 1 ½ bath
1,446 square feet
Built in 1906
Status: was C, sold as B

#25   3 bedroom / 1 bath
955 square feet
Built in 1911
Status: was C, now B-

#26   3 bedroom / 1 bath
1,554 square feet
Built in 1919
Status: was C, now C+

#27   3 bedroom / 1 bath
768 square feet
Built in 1947
Status: was C+, now B

#28 5 bedroom / 2 bath
1,703 square feet
Built in 1985
Status: was D, now C+

#29 3 bedroom / 1 bath
1,360 square feet
Built in 1941
Status: was B, now B

#30 2 bedroom / 1 bath
848 square feet
Built in 1918
Status: was D, now C

#31 5 bedroom / 2 bath
1,600 square feet
Built in 1949
Status: was C, now B

#32 4 bedroom / 1 bath
1,216 square feet
Built in 1971
Status: was C, now B

#33 2+ bedroom / 1 bath
991 square feet
Built in 1944
Status: was C, now B

#34 3 bedroom / 1 bath
1,113 square feet
Built in 1928
Status: was C, now B

#35 (4) 2 bedroom / 1 bath
Apartments
700 square feet per unit
Built in 1975
Status: was C, now B

#36   3 bedroom / 1 bath
       1,294 square feet
       Built in 1908
       Status: was C, now B

#37   5 bedroom / 2.75 bath
       2,840 square feet
       Built in 1928
       Status: was C, now B

#38   3 bedroom / 1 bath
       1,443 square feet
       Built in 1945
       Status: was C, now C

#39   (4) 2 bedroom / 1 bath
       Apartments
       700 square feet per unit
       Built in 1975
       Status: was C, now B

#40 3 bedroom / 1 bath
792 square feet
Built in 1920
Status: was C, now B

#41 3 bedroom / 1 bath
1,168 square feet
Built in 1958
Status: was B, now A

#42 2 bedroom / 1 bath
616 square feet
Built in 1930
Status: was D, sold as D

#43 3 bedroom / 1 bath
1,260 square feet
Built in 1907
Status: was D, now C+

#44   3 bedroom / 1 bath
1,360 square feet
Built in 1969
Status: was C, now B

#45   4 bedroom / 1 bath
1,508 square feet
Built in 1890
Status: was D, sold as B

#46   3 bedroom / 1 bath
1,264 square feet
Built in 1905
Status: was C, now B

#47   3 bedroom / 1 bath
1,404 square feet
Built in 1909
Status: was C, now B

#48   2 bedroom / 1 bath
744 square feet
Built in 1943
Status: was D, now B

#49   4+ bedroom / 1 bath
1,544 square feet
Built in 1904
Status: was C, now C

#50   2 bedroom / 1 bath
804 square feet
Built in 1940
Status: was C, now C

#51   4 bedroom / 2 bath
1,538 square feet
Built in 1907
Status: was C, now C

#52   3 bedroom / 1 bath
1,260 square feet
Built in 1937
Status: was C, now A

#53   3 bedroom / 1 bath
1,200 square feet
Built in 1946
Status: was C, sold as C+

#54   2 bedroom / 1 bath
856 square feet
Built in 1908
Status: was D-, sold as C

#55   2 bedroom / 1 bath
936 square feet
Built in 1907
Status: was C, now C

#56 2 bedroom / 1 bath
1,016 square feet
Built in 1915
Status: was C, now C

#57 3 bedroom / 1 bath
1,393 square feet
Built in 1948
Status: was C, now B

#58 3 bedroom / 1 bath
992 square feet
Built in 1953
Status: was C, now B

#59 (2) 3 bedroom / 1 bath
Condo's
932 square feet per unit
Built in 1969
Status: was C, now B

Flipped Out?

#60 (2) 3 bedroom / 1 bath
Condo's
932 square feet per unit
Built in 1969
Status: was C, now B

#61 4 bedroom / 2 bath
2112 square feet
Built in 1939
Status: was C, now B

#62 4 bedroom / 2 bath
1,788 square feet
Built in 1952
Status: was C, now B

#63 (2) 3 bedroom / 1 bath
units
932 square feet per unit
Built in 1969
Status: was C, now B

#64   4 bedroom / 1 bath
1,694 square feet
Built in 1925
Status: was C, now C

#65   2 bedroom / 1 bath
1,064 square feet
Built in 1955
Status: was C, now B

#66   3 bedroom / 2 ½ bath
1,557 square feet
Built 2007
Status: was B+, now B+

#67   5 bedroom / 1 ¾ bath
1,860 square feet
Built in 1922
Status: was C, now B

#68   4 bedroom / 1 ¾   bath
1,520 square feet
Built in 1904
Status: was C, now C

#69   2 bedroom / 1 bath
832 square feet
Built in 1903
Status: was C, now B

#70   3 bedroom / 1 bath
1,266 square feet
Built in 1954
Status: was A, now A

#71   3 bedroom / 1 bath
1,012 square feet
Built in 1955
Status: was C, now A

#72 1 bedroom / 1 bath
600 square feet
Built in 1950
Status: was D, now C+

#73 3 bedroom / 1 bath
1,148 square feet
Built in 1926
Status: was C, now B

#74 3 bedroom / 1 bath
668 square feet
Built in 1943
Status: was C, now B

#75 1 bedroom / 1 bath
582 square feet
Built in 1910
Status: was C, now C+

#76 (3) 2 bedroom / 1 ½
bath Apartments
965 square feet per unit
Built in 1977
Status: was B, now B

#77 3+ bedroom / 1 bath
1,440 square feet
Built in 1905
Status: was C, now B

#78 3 bedroom / 1 bath
1,501 square feet
Built in 1925
Status: was B, now A

#79 3 bedroom / 1 bath
1,257 square feet
Built in 1916
Status: was C, now C

#80 4 bedroom / 1 bath
1,395 square feet
Built in 1905
Status: was B, now A

#81 4 bedroom / 1 bath
1,152 square feet
Built in 1972
Status: was B, now A

#82 4 bedroom / 1 bath
1,424 square feet
Built in 1917
Status: was B, now B

#83 4 bedroom / 1 bath
1,377 square feet
Built in 1925
Status: was B-, now B

#84 (2) 3 bedroom / 1 ½ bath
Condo's
1123 square feet per unit
Built in 1969
Status: was C, now B

#85 3 bedroom / 2 bath
1,252 square feet
Built in 1989
Status: was B, now A

DIRECT ORDER FORM

E-mail orders: mike@sandersoninc.com
Postal orders: PO Box 111821
                  Tacoma, WA 98411
Website: www.SandersonInc.com

Please send _____ copies of the book, FLIPPED OUT? at $34.95 U.S. per copy.

Name _____

Address _____

City _____ State _____ Zip Code _____

Telephone _____

E-mail address _____

Sales Tax: Please add 8.8% for products shipped to Washington addresses.

Shipping by USPS Priority Mail
             U.S.A. $5 for the first book
                        $3 for each additional book.

             International: $10 for the first book
                        $6 for each additional book (estimate).

Payment: ❑   Check   ❑   Credit Card

Card number _____

Name on card _____ Exp. _____

Billing address _____

Website _____

LET MIKE HELP YOU BUILD YOUR REAL ESTATE BUSINESS

Mike Sanderson can help you build your real estate investment business from the bottom up in a format you're most comfortable with.

- Mike is available in person, in real time for consultation, speaking and training individually or in groups. For personal attention, please email him at Mike @SandersonInc.com.
- Mike is also available on the web at www.SandersonInc.com where you can find more helpful information, speaking schedules, training opportunities, new book announcements, and online ordering of print books, ebooks and other Sanderson Inc. materials and presentations.

Here are some typical examples of how Mike has wound up helping people:

Example 1: Often It's Better to Just Say No

". . . Jim pulls me aside at the end of a real estate investors meeting saying he needs some help with a house. Describing a house he is considering purchasing, it seems he has the numbers figured out and is pretty close to pulling the trigger on the purchase. He also appears to be a little surprised by some of the questions I am asking him. Such as, what do you want to accomplish with this house? What is the goal? What do you need help with?

After a little further discussion, I agreed to meet him at the house to look at what opportunities I saw. Walking through the house there were a few minor concerns, but the real problem arose when I pointed out the lack of opportunity in the project. As I walked the house with him, it was evident that the house was at its highest and best use already. This left no room for him to add value now or in the future. When Jim then asked me if I would do the project, I said no for the very reason I just described. I explained this position very carefully, as I have done many times before with other investors, because it is not my intention to discourage them but rather to help them. There was absolutely nothing wrong with Jim purchasing that house for part of his rental portfolio, but he needed to know that there was no room for error either. He needed to realize that what he would be buying was at its highest and best use right now. In this particular case, Jim took my advice and decided to keep looking for other opportunities based on our walk through. . .”

Example Two: Why Isn't It All About the House?
“. . . A few years ago I was involved with a small group of investors from the Seattle area. This group was primarily focused on property acquisition and financing techniques. I learned a lot and got to know many of the participants.

One day, several of these folks got together and inquired if they could see my operation. I agreed to have them down to my office and take a look at a couple of my projects that were in progress. This being my first experience with a group like this, I wasn't sure what to expect. When they arrived, we spent a lot more time at one of my projects than I had expected with me answering questions one right after another. A few of the questions were: Why did you move the laundry room?; how did you decide to arrange the kitchen like that?; and when replacing the windows, how did you decide which ones open or not?

These all were very good questions and they all had one theme in common, once we acquire the house, what potential does it have as an investment? They had never been exposed to what I was showing them. As investors, they had spent most of their time studying financing and acquisition techniques and in doing so had bypassed analyzing all of the opportunity that exists within the house itself. I was giving them their first look through the landlord's set of glasses I wear all the time – in short, the existing potential in the house and how to add value after the purchase. All the acquisition, financing and numerical analysis still leaves you without that the important piece I specialize in --the investment opportunities within the house itself.

This experience was memorable because it was the first time I asked myself -- why isn't it all about the house? . . ."

Example Three: There Is So Much More Than The Numbers

" . . . There is so much more you should know about the house than just the numbers. When the Microsoft executive pulled me aside to ask more about the discussion that had taken place that evening concerning contractors, it was a little uncomfortable at first. Here is a man who has advanced college degrees, knows the financial game and numbers like the back of his hand asking me for advice on a house he already owns. I was a little intimidated to say the least. Fortunately for me, this same gentleman quickly put me at ease and I found myself educating him about the structural components of a house that I learned as a teenager. In retrospect, as strange as this may seem, I admired him for seeking the knowledge he needed to know."

Example Four: We Are Different, But So Much The Same

"I have met with property management companies and assisted many of them in improving their business. In these situations, I find myself asking questions about what situations they are in and the basic philosophies they run their business by. For the most part, their management procedures are run through set procedures, but it is the human relations challenges they need assistance with -- namely the relationships they have with property owners, their staff and contractors. I offer a unique value to these property managers when it comes to resolving people problems as I deal with these kinds of issues all day long, every day. Their situation is a little different from mine in that they have more people involved in their transactions, but by in large, their business has many similar features as mine does, so I find that I can use my experiences to help them get their businesses to where they want it to be."

For help in building your real estate investment business, contact Mike Sanderson at Mike@SandersonInc.com.